The conservataria
320.52 Coo

Silver City Public Library

D0976719

The

CONSERVATARIAN

MANIFESTO

The

CONSERVATARIAN

MANIFESTO

LIBERTARIANS, CONSERVATIVES,

and the Fight for the Right's Future

CHARLES C. W. COOKE

SILVER CITY PUBLIC LIBRARY
515 W. COLLEGE AVE.
SILVER CITY, NM 88061

CROWN
FORUM
NEW YORK

320.52
Coo
$25⁰⁰
4/15

0266915

Copyright © 2015 by Charles C. W. Cooke

All rights reserved.
Published in the United States by Crown Forum,
an imprint of the Crown Publishing Group,
a division of Random House LLC,
a Penguin Random House Company, New York.
www.crownpublishing.com

CROWN FORUM with colophon is a registered
trademark of Random House LLC.

Library of Congress Cataloging-in-Publication Data
Cooke, Charles C. W.
  The conservatarian manifesto : libertarians, conservatives, and the
fight for the right's future / Charles C. W. Cooke. — First edition.
    pages cm
1. Conservatism—United States. 2. Libertarianism—United States.
I. Title.

  JC573.2.U6C666 2015
  320.520973—dc23

                          2014031658

ISBN 978-0-8041-3972-4
eBook ISBN 978-0-8041-3973-1

Printed in the United States of America

Jacket design by Jessica Morphew

10 9 8 7 6 5 4 3 2 1

First Edition

To my father, Phillip,
who is everything that I aspire to be

Contents

The

CONSERVATARIAN

MANIFESTO

Introduction

ON my desk at *National Review*, there is a piece of cardboard that was mailed to me by a man who is no great admirer of my work. "Conservatism SUCKS!" it declares in erratically scrawled capital letters. "Let's get really conservative and go back to pre–Magna Carta days!"

This is a jab to which I have grown accustomed in the past few years, based as it is on a popular misapprehension as to what those of us on the Right actually believe. It is worth clearing up this error at the start. That in America the friends of liberty are called "conservatives" and the centralizing authoritarians are referred to as "liberals" is one of the great semantic jokes of history. In almost every other part of the world, rightward-leaning political movements seek primarily to conserve the long-established order, and in consequence compete not for meaningful ideological terrain but for stewardship and for stasis. Elections abroad tend to be narrow and meretricious affairs, in which minor reductions in the considerable power of the state take on great significance and "philosophy" is seen as a dirty, even dangerous, word.

In the United States, by happy contrast, conservatism is marked by its unorthodoxy and its radicalism. Conservatives are passionate and ambitious, and their concern is for neither the international norms nor the tribal precepts that have animated most of human history, but for the manifestation of eccentric ideas that have surfaced only recently—among them property rights; separation of powers; hard limits on the power of the state; staunch protections of the rights of conscience, assembly, speech, privacy, and self-protection; a preference for local governance over central planning; a free and dynamic market economy that permits rapid change and remarkable innovation; and, above all, a distrust of any government that would step in to answer questions that can be better resolved by civil society.

Insofar as conservatives look back into the past, they typically do so to reestablish their purchase on timeless truths about the nature of politics and of human beings and to reacquaint themselves with a subversive political framework that—although more than two centuries old—has been the most effective steward of political progress and material improvement in human history. So accustomed have we in the West become to the blessings of ordered liberty that it can be tempting to believe that this is the natural order of things. Alas, it is not. Thomas Jefferson, the principal author of the Declaration of Independence, correctly observed that "the natural progress of things is for liberty to yield, and government to gain ground," adding wisely that freedoms, once lost, are rarely regained. But he did not mention that enjoying liberty in the first instance is a rare privilege indeed—one that has been accorded to only a handful of the billions of people who have come and gone from the Earth. If conservatism in America has one goal, it is to preserve that opportunity.

This country's founding generation was preoccupied with designing a system that would prove difficult for evil and ambitious men to commandeer—not because there was an uncommonly large number of such men here in the late eighteenth century, but because history had shown them to be a feature of every age and a threat to all peoples. For most of the country's history, my colleague Kevin D. Williamson notes, "politics" has been the word used to describe the altercation between those laboring under the impression that "our institutions could be channels of moral action and reliably ethical arbiters of such ill-defined standards as 'fairness' and 'social justice,' if only we put the right people in power," and those who believe that "man is a fallen creature" who cannot always be trusted to act rationally and magnanimously. This question, of the essential nature of man, is at the very root of the disagreement between the Left and the Right—the Right's skepticism resting heavily upon the presumption that human beings do not change when they are accorded great power and that, if anything, we should be more and not less suspicious of anybody who seeks out influence; the Left taking the opposing view.

The Right's acknowledgment of the limitations of man and of the state that he has created is imperative. It is often asserted that free markets perform better than does central preparation, and that governments are unable to achieve by design what a free people may spontaneously. But it is rarely explained *why* this is the case. The answer is refreshingly simple: Because so much that the state does it is not designed to do well, however ingenious are the men and women we put in charge. Brilliant as our bureaucrats may be, they are simply incapable of running a country this size. As George Will discerned in 2014, the United States "is not a parcel to be 'taken' anywhere. It is the spontaneous order of 316 million people making billions of daily decisions, cooperatively contracting together, moving the country in gloriously unplanned directions." It does not matter whether we have a Harvard professor or a business mogul or a lifelong politico running the Department of Energy; none of them can do half as well for a local in Springfield, Virginia, as that local can do for himself. It does not matter how accomplished or credentialed the economists at the head of the Department of Commerce are; they will never grasp the details of the market better than the businesses they are seeking to aid. All too often, our politics is focused on a rotten capital city that sits on the Eastern Seaboard and not on our various institutions of meaning: the churches, charities, clubs, associations, sports teams, businesses, families, towns, cities, counties, and states that make up the whole. This vexes conservatives, at least ostensibly. But they might do more with their aggravation the next time they are in a position of power, steadfastly resisting the temptation merely to replace one set of tsars with another and choosing, this time, actually to let go.

There *will* be such a time. That the United States remains so keenly politically divided—and that its conservatives have not yet given up—is a matter of great disappointment to social democrats and a source of considerable inspiration to me and to many millions of others. In the United States, questions that were long ago settled in Europe and beyond serve as matters of daily deliberation. Among those questions: "What role should the government play in health care?" "Should the national government take a leading or a limited role in the national economy?" "Are individuals to be trusted with their own protection and allowed to possess the tools with which they might defend themselves?"

The scholar Francis Fukuyama, who in the mid-1990s declared that history had come to an end, seems now to be disappointed that its contributors are still kicking. Lamenting rather hysterically in 2013 that America's exceptional character was "not necessarily a good thing," Fukuyama spoke for many progressives when he observed that in the rest of the world, "the losing side of the election generally accepts the right of the majority to govern and does not seek to use every institutional lever available to undermine the winner." Not so in America, where change is slow and the losers are afforded ample opportunity to regroup and to push their ideas. Fleshing out his objections, Fukuyama turned recently to Obamacare, proposing that

> *only in America can a government mandate to buy some-*
> *thing that is good for you in any case be characterized as*
> *an intolerable intrusion on individual liberty. According*
> *to many Republicans, Obamacare signals nothing short*
> *of the end of the United States, something that "we will*
> *never recover from," in the words of one GOP House*

*member. . . . It is this kind of rhetoric that makes non-
Americans scratch their heads in disbelief.*

Let them scratch. It should be clear by now that any genuine diversity of thought will naturally produce both good
and bad results. As Fukuyama himself concedes, the same
structural and cultural frameworks that have allowed a genuine political opposition to prosper have also "slowed down
or prevented the growth of a large, European-style regula-
tory welfare state, allowing the private sector to flourish and
unleashing the United States as a world leader in technology
and entrepreneurship."

Fukuyama and his ilk underestimate the virtue of the
space that government retrenchment leaves, and do not understand that preventing the metastasis of the state has more
benefits than just *economic* dynamism. Governments are unlike most private enterprise, which must stand or fall by its
merits, and unlike civil society, which survives only by convincing volunteers that their time is being well spent. Able to
recruit an almost endless stream of treasure and violence to its
cause, Washington makes mistakes that live on for decades—
becoming petrified by the self-interested and then wrapped
for the electorate in warm language and vague sentiment that
has little to do with the actual consequences of whatever is
being discussed. Having a movement that opposes much of
this in principle is not an annoyance; it is a prerequisite for
liberty.

The Tea Party and libertarian contingents, both of
which are perpetually rolling their eyes at mainstream Republicans and their allies, have done the broader movement a

great service by demanding that such power as the ostensible champions of limited government enjoy is to be leveraged in service of reform. Those elements have been right, too, to observe that the conservatives whose idea of change is simply to replace the management have abandoned a core American principle: That there is only so much that the state can, and *should*, do. Some among this group have become sufficiently frustrated with their brothers-in-arms to have established new and discrete groups, even abandoning or amending the "conservative" and "libertarian" labels traditionally used to describe the two strongest building blocks of the Right's co-alition. These are the "conservatarians" referred to in the title of this book, and they have an important point to make.

But not an exhaustive one. *Pace* George Washington, parties and ideologies can be extraordinarily useful organizing tools, and those who dismiss them out of hand tend to ignore the fact that the cabal and the clique are as inevitable as is politics itself. Nonetheless, however virtuous or natural they might be, all organizations are at risk of stagnation and calcification, and range from time to time into the danger of losing their souls and their appeal. On drugs, on gay marriage, on defense, and on the structure of the government—to name just a few areas in which the Right is unself-reflective—conservatives have all too often tended to rely upon reflexive justifications that they might never accept in other areas, opening themselves up to charges of hypocrisy and weakening their case with both their natural allies and with the independent voters that have customarily been the key to their success. This, I will suggest, is a dangerous mistake.

This is a book about a party and a philosophy that, in a number of areas, has lost its way. It is a book about change but also about tradition; a book that is sometimes critical but ultimately optimistic; a book that, at its heart, appreciates the age-old truths that man is not capable of perfection, that what cannot go on forever will stop, and that there are no solutions, only trade-offs; and a book that attempts to apply those timeless principles to the present day.

It is a book that offers the good news that most of what ails America can—and by rights *should*—be fixed by the conservative movement. Conservatives remain keenly in touch with the principles that have led the country to its present position of plenty and of international primacy, but of late they have exhibited a nasty habit of focusing on the wrong things and ignoring what it was that catapulted them to a position of influence in the first place.

These mistakes have not been fatal. The supposedly ebullient progressive moment of 2012 was, it turns out, little more than a mirage—a particularly turbulent swing of the pendulum that benefited but did not solidify the Left's agenda. Barack Obama and his philosophy have not captured the American heart.

Nor, alas, have conservatives. But, I will argue, they *can*. In particular, I hope to remind the American Right that ours is an iconoclastic movement. I do not, of course, have all the answers. Nobody does. But I hope, at least, to start an argument within the group and to force conservatives to reexamine some of their basic principles and to question why they support what they support. There is limited virtue in merely restating the case against one's opponents, and I have no intention of doing so here. If you are looking for a straight-up polemic, then I suggest you buy a different book. If, perchance, you are interested in a reappraisal of the conservative movement that seeks to leave it ever more vital and more closely in touch with the timeless principles that have guided it to this point, I hope you will find here something of use.

1

WHAT'S WRONG WITH
CONSERVATIVES?

———

BARACK Obama's reelection to the presidency was met with the hyperbole, panic, and unchecked euphoria that is typical of the Washington press corps. As morning broke on November 7, 2012, and the political class took stock of what had happened, a claim swiftly rose to the surface: Progressivism was now the dominant political philosophy in America, and conservatism as we had known it was dead. Obama's victory, MSNBC's Ari Melber wrote breathlessly in the *Huffington Post*, was "the most decisive mandate for an assertive, progressive governing model in well over a generation."

Melber's view was the regnant one, at least initially. In a hasty postmortem piece simply titled "Welcome to Liberal America," Ben Smith and Zeke Miller predicted on the pop-culture blog *BuzzFeed* that "this is the country, and the Republican Party has to adapt." The president's rehiring, the pair contended, licensed him to "carry, if not quite fulfill, a liberal vision of activist government and soft but sometimes deadly power abroad that will define his party for a generation."

Politics being a zero-sum game, the prevailing take was that the Republican Party was destined to go the way of the Whigs—powerless in the face of demographic change, unable to match the unassailable Democratic coalition, and years behind a deep-seated ideological switch that had pushed the United States away from the center right and toward the temptations of social democracy. If the GOP continued on its course, it would end up as a rump regional party. Sure, if the Republicans made some leftward changes and rode the political pendulum, they would likely hold office in the future. But they would not effect substantial change. Like conservative parties in other countries, the role of Republicans in American life would henceforth be to manage the welfare state better than does the Left, to slow the pace of change, and to blunt the sharper excesses of a dominant progressivism.

Elsewhere, the election victory was regarded as a likely overture to more radical social alterations: comprehensive immigration reform, tax increases, the nationalization of gay marriage, stricter gun control, the legalization of marijuana, drastic reductions in carbon emissions, and the entrenchment of Obamacare were all on the horizon. From wherever he is, the late British prime minister Harold Macmillan must have smiled a wry smile. When asked what he feared most in politics, Macmillan famously—perhaps apocryphally—replied, "Events, dear boy, events." To have driven home the point, he might have added, "and the passage of time."

It is probably inevitable that presidents' second terms will collapse into themselves—frayed at the edges by the shifting sands of coalitions; racked by scandals, the consequences of which can be put off for only so long; and slowed in their momentum by the media's tendency to always be looking for the next big thing. There is nothing special about our own era, and despite the reverent and deferential manner in which Barack Obama's apologists continue to talk of him, our 44th president has not bucked this trend. In all likelihood, he will not. In his sixth year as the head of the executive branch, Barack Obama is as unpopular as was George W. Bush in the same period, is so lacking in political capital that he has been reduced to the indignities of executive action, and has been forced to watch as his signature legislative achievement, the Affordable Care Act, has become a dead weight around his party's weakening neck.

Obama is now enmeshed in scandals involving the IRS, the NSA, the Department of Justice, the Department of State, the Department of Veterans Affairs, and the INS (Immigration and Naturalization Service). He is being investigated from many corners and sued, successfully, from others. Most important, perhaps, he is discovering that his legislative and philosophical platform has not taken root in any permanent sense—and, I would venture, *cannot* take root in any permanent sense. The areas in which the president has chosen to focus—health care, immigration, gun control, and climate change—barely register on the list of citizens' concerns. Meanwhile, his abject lack of interest in foreign affairs is proving costly to his reputation (and that of America) and to the stability of the world. His base, once deeply in love with him and what he appeared to represent, is mostly unenthused. Across the country, ambitious Democrats are determined to distance themselves from the president, turning down opportunities to appear with him at campaign stops and taking harsh swipes at his agenda in a manner that would have been unthinkable just a few years back.

Rather than serving as the overture to a brave new era, it now seems that the period 2008–2012 was, in fact, the high-water mark of progressive electoral and legislative success. For two years, the Democratic Party had an all but free hand, enjoying a popular president in the White House, strong control of the House of Representatives, and a filibuster-proof majority in the Senate. By 2015, the tide has turned almost completely. Now, Republicans boast their largest majority in the House since World War II, are comfortably in charge of the Senate, and are continuing to dominate politics at the state and local levels. What could possibly have happened?

Lost in all the drama of November 7, 2012, was a crucial detail: That while voters preferred Barack Obama to Mitt Romney, they did not necessarily buy his *ideology*. Shortly after the election, *The New Republic*'s Timothy Noah tried to break down the exit polling to get a solid impression of what had just happened. Frustrated, he threw his hands up, griping that "the exercise [proved] weirdly difficult."

On first glance it is indeed perplexing. Six in ten voters considered the economy to be the most important issue, seven out of ten voters considered that economy to be in dire straits, and a majority of voters trusted Romney more than Obama as an economic steward. And yet . . . Obama won. A majority disagreed with the president that taxes on people with incomes above $250,000 should be raised—a promise that Obama had repeatedly and publicly made. And yet, Obama won. A majority favored repealing Obamacare *completely*—a promise that Mitt Romney made the centerpiece of his campaign. And yet Obama won. A majority thought the country was "on the wrong track" and that "government does too much," and only one-quarter of respondents said that their families' financial situations were getting better.

And yet . . . well, you get the idea.

To paraphrase Smith and Miller, then: "this [the election result] is *not* the country." To rebut Ari Melber, this is *not* the most decisive mandate for an assertive, progressive governing model in well over a generation. It's a mess.

Conservatives should be pleased about this. But not *too* pleased. For while the president and his legislative agenda are disliked by a majority, so too are the Republican Party and its agenda. And, arguably, people dislike Republicans much, much more. Worse still, the recent memories of Republicans in power are not happy ones. The march of time may be rehabilitating George W. Bush's reputation. But his years are still viewed unfavorably by most. Meanwhile, people under the age of thirty hold no warm memories of Ronald Reagan, of economic resurgence driven by deregulation, and of Cold War victory. For them, the most admired president of the past few decades is Bill Clinton. Obama may be on his way out, and Americans may have learned once more that the trailer is often better than the movie. But that doesn't mean the old guard is on its way back in.

Before the GOP will be trusted again as the natural party of government, it will have to rebuild—and dramatically. During the Bush administration's turbulent eight years, the Republican Party steadily ruined its reputation, damaging the public conception of conservatism in the process. Republicans spent too much, subsidized too much, spied too much, and controlled too much. The party abandoned its core principle of federalism, undermined free trade, favored the interests of big businesses over genuinely free markets, used government power to push social issues too aggressively, and, ultimately, was somewhat co-opted by the Christian Right, which moved from being one part of the coalition to being the dominant one. Most of all, the Republican Party lost its reputation for fiscal restraint, constitutional propriety, and mastery of foreign affairs. That conservatives were tempted to use power to get what they wanted when they held power is understandable. Life is easier when your man is in the White House. But government does not cease to be destructive because the men in charge carry the letter "R" after their names, and the willingness of many conservatives to abandon their principles the very moment that they wrapped their grubby hands around the levers of power has contributed to a reasonable suspicion that the Right's objection to the use of government as an agent of social change is situational. If it is to win again, it will have to demonstrate that it is not merely agitating for a different form of Leviathan.

Alas, in a number of key areas, Republicans are still making the same mistakes. If they continue to do so, they will not only continue to give their party a bad name, they will convince the public that the very notion of liberty deserves a bad name, too. For the United States and for the world, this would be catastrophic.

AMONG the fashionable set, an article of faith has lately been consecrated: The GOP has become "extreme" and is running away from the political center and into unelectable territory. This claim has little but rhetoric to recommend it. Certainly, Republicans today are more conservative than they were during the Bush years. As a result of world events over which he had no control, and of a personal philosophy that infamously held that "if someone is hurting, the government must move," President Bush moved the GOP onto unfamiliar ground, injuring the party's historically positive foreign policy record and quixotically attempting to win over new constituencies with a series of domestic spending initiatives that were anathema to the rhetorical and political norms of the movement. But this was the exception, not the rule. It is *Bush*'s party— not the one of today—that is the aberration.

In the era of Ronald Reagan and George H. W. Bush, the Republican Party reduced taxes, cut regulations, and relentlessly attacked the popular conceit that the answer to the nation's problems was invariably more government intervention. And the Republicans who followed—the class of rebels that arguably ruined Bill Clinton's presidency—were perhaps even more conservative than was Reagan. These were the movers and shakers who created the "Contract with America"—the brash kids who in 1994 seized upon President Clinton's overreach on health care and on gun control and took over the House of Representatives, promising to abolish a host of federal departments, to nix almost one hundred government programs, to pass a Constitutional amendment requiring a balanced budget, to slash the welfare rolls substantially, and to push powers back to the states. Sound familiar? It should. Today the Republican Party has merely moved back to its former position.

Its opponents have shifted, too. Following the brief Clintonian hiatus that was brought about in part by the conscious desire to again win the White House and in part by the realities and opportunities presented by a divided government, Democrats have returned to their favored post-1968 position on the far Left. The Democratic Leadership Council, once an influential and moderating force, has been abolished. The party has picked up positions on abortion, health care, religious liberty, and gun control that most Americans consider to be severe. It has made Obamacare—a law that most Americans did not want and *still do not want*—the centerpiece of its time in power. In 1996, Bill Clinton announced that "the era of big government is over." The very notion of a Democrat saying those words today should make you snort derisively.

Taken together, the Republicans' move back to the Right and the Democrats' move back to the Left have created an illusion: that conservatives have become radicals in the second decade of the twenty-first century. But illusions are not to be trusted.

DESPITE all of the Right's energy over the past fifty years—and a good deal of electoral success to boot—the basic assumptions of the American government have in no meaningful sense been reversed. One of the *New York Times*'s two conservatives, Ross Douthat, has described a "deep, abiding gulf between the widespread conservative idea of what a true Conservative Moment would look like and the mainstream idea of the same." His case is a simple one: That while Ronald Reagan and his offspring managed to halt the march of the progressive movement and to publicly embarrass the more radical components of its agenda, they never succeeded in undoing the damage to limited government that had been done in the 1930s and 1960s. "To liberals and many moderates," Douthat observes,

> *it often seems like the right gets what it wants in these arguments and then just gets more extreme, demanding cuts atop cuts, concessions atop concessions, deregulation upon deregulation, tax cuts upon tax cuts. But to many conservatives, the right has never come remotely close to getting what it actually wants, whether in the Reagan era or the Gingrich years or now the age of the Tea Party—because what it wants is an actually smaller government, as opposed to one that just grows somewhat more slowly than liberals and the left would like.*

Allied with this misconception—that conservatives have "won" in any serious ideological sense in the past century—is the peculiar but popular delusion that the government can realistically be called "small." To my eyes, and to those of many of my brothers-in-arms, the federal government is a vast, intrusive, unwieldy, undemocratic, bureaucratic disaster that never stops feeding, and that is slowly but surely dismantling the beautiful and necessary ideas of the American Founding in the name of a utopian future that never arrives. Nevertheless, each time that conservatives so much as hint at trimming back the rate of growth—not even cutting the budget in absolute terms, just slowing the rate of increase—they are immediately met with wailing, gnashing of teeth, and the risible and brazen insistence that the poor will die in the streets and the elderly will starve to death outside Denny's.

"The sequester," George Will wrote drily in 2013, "forced liberals to clarify their conviction that whatever the government's size is at any moment, it is the bare minimum necessary to forestall intolerable suffering." Rarely have truer words been spoken. The *New York Times*, which rather smugly regards itself as being America's putative "newspaper of record," loses its collective mind each and every time that there is even the slightest challenge to the status quo. In October 2013, on day six of the government shutdown, the Pulitzer Prize–winning columnist Maureen Dowd penned a risibly overwrought column titled "A Place Once Called Washington," in which she looked forward to 2084 and described a scene "in the capital of the land formerly called North America." Dowd imagined apes sitting where the Lincoln Memorial once stood, and Washington, D.C.'s "once beautiful boulevards" being "now strewn with the detritus of democracy, scraps of the original Constitution, corroded White House ID cards, stacks of worthless bills tumbling out of the Treasury Department . . . Because there was no clean [spending] bill," Dowd narrated, "now there is only a filthy stench."

Whatever one's view of the wisdom of our current trench

warfare and the political forces that have caused it, it takes an impressively fertile imagination to regard the government's shutting down for the eighteenth time in four decades as a crisis of historical proportions—especially when one acknowledges that it continued to operate at 83 percent capacity, and that the House offered repeatedly to fund almost every part of the government in the interim and to furnish *all* parts of the government with the requested cash if Obamacare was delayed for just a single year.

It is this sort of ahistorical hysteria that has also led to progressives declaring routinely that, since conservatives have "destroyed the New Deal," the Left's efforts to grow the government actually amount to a heroic defense of the "last scraps of the welfare state." Given that government spending on social programs is at its zenith, this, too, is patently absurd. Fifty years ago, the claim that America prioritized defense over welfare—or "guns over butter," to borrow a phrase from a bad man—had some truth to it. In 1953, defense spending accounted for 54 percent of the federal budget and social spending represented only 26 percent. Given that defense is the primary role of government—and especially of the federal government—there was, of course, nothing wrong with this. But by the time of President Obama's inauguration, the ratio of spending had been flipped somewhat dramatically. In 2009, social spending accounted for 61 percent of the federal budget, whereas defense took just 22 percent.

The change that took place in the latter half of the twentieth century was not temporary, but *structural*. In all likelihood, it is not going to be altered anytime soon. This, sadly, is the path that we have chosen. Federal taxes could be raised to record levels, the property of all millionaires could be summarily confiscated, and the entire Department of Defense could be eliminated, but if we continue on our present course, our social spending would still bankrupt the federal government. As Doug Elmendorf, director of the Congressional Budget Office (CBO), wrote in 2011,

> *one big challenge in bringing spending down is the fact that the rising costs of health care and the aging of the population are working in the opposite direction, pushing spending up for major government programs as they are currently structured. Largely because of those trends, spending on Social Security and the major health programs is projected to rise from 8.7 percent of GDP in 2007 to 12.2 percent in 2021. (The expansion of federal outlays for health insurance coverage in last year's health care legislation plays a smaller role in that increase.)*

Elmendorf went on to explain that, if the United States insists upon making no significant changes to social spending, defense and other federal outlays would have to be reduced by a whopping 60 percent by 2021 *just to keep the budget where it was in 2011*. He finished his post with a warning, writing that "we as a society will either have to pay more for our government, accept less in government services and benefits, or both. . . . For many people, none of those choices is appealing—but they cannot be avoided for very long."

Whether they can or not, a significant number of people in America seem determined to pretend that there is no problem at hand. Witness, for instance, the *New York Times* editorial board's astonishing 2013 reaction to a Republican proposal to cut the food stamp budget by a paltry $40 billion over ten years. This "turning of the screw," the board contended, was "intolerable," "cruel," "mindless," and even a "national embarrassment." Never mind that the House had suggested cutting by 5 percent a program that had expanded by 70 percent in the five years during which Barack Obama had been president—and which would continue to expand. Never mind that the Congressional Budget Office had reported that, despite its extremely modest cuts, the bill would actually *increase* spending over the next decade by 57 percent—pushing up to $725 billion a program that had cost $461.7 billion in the previous ten years. Never mind all that. Republicans had dared to suggest even the most modest of fiscal restraint, and in the twenty-first century, that is heresy.

Over the past half-century, America's progressives have managed successfully to export to the general public a perverted conception of morality in which forever advocating short-term gain at the expense of long-term solvency is somehow a sign of "compassion" and in which reality is expected to bend to meet good intentions and glib slogans and never to break in consequence. It is possible, if not probable, that the fiscal time bomb on which Americans now sit will eventually be solved with a "grand bargain"—a bipartisan moment in which both sides hold their noses and usher in a mixture of tax increases and spending cuts sufficient to avoid calamity. But whatever the mixture of those two variables is, cuts such as the one the Republican Party proposed to the food stamp program will have to be a routine and unremarkable feature of America's fiscal future.

There was a time when we at least agreed on that. Now, the most familiar newspaper in the country cannot seem to wrap its head around it. Nor, apparently, can the political class. The subjugation of outcomes to intentions is by no means a new political tendency, but prior to the Obama presidency it was generally agreed upon by both sides that our mounting debt and unsustainable entitlements spending represented a grave problem. Politicians may well have disagreed as to how the United States might best deal with that challenge, but they didn't pretend it didn't exist. Which is to say that the notion that spending beyond one's means, expressed best perhaps by Charles Dickens in *David Copperfield*, remained uncontroversial:

> *"My other piece of advice, Copperfield," said Mr. Micawber, "you know. Annual income twenty pounds, annual expenditure nineteen nineteen and six, result happiness. Annual income twenty pounds, annual expenditure twenty pounds ought and six, result misery."*

From this timeless passage, conservatives should perhaps take heart. Economic gravity cannot be defied for too long, and wishful thinking and hyperbole will get their practitioners only so far before they run up against a brick wall. Somewhere in their bones, the American people seem to have taken notice. James Stimson, author of a mathematical model that seeks to track Americans' "policy mood," proposed in 2012 that the electorate is currently more conservative than it has been at any point since Dwight Eisenhower was first elected in 1952. This, one suspects, is no accident.

Exit polls from 2012 show that while the public tends to agree with conservatives more on questions of economics, it still blames George W. Bush for the financial crisis—and by a significant margin. Eventually, this will pass. By the time Barack Obama is done with his eight years, it will be almost impossible for anyone to continue to blame a man who left office two terms back—even if they wish to. When Obama's moment is over, Republicans must make sure that they are ready to step into the gap. Simply waiting it out will not suffice. Instead, Republicans must reestablish themselves as the party of liberty, demonstrating to a skeptical but interested electorate that they are committed to laissez-faire; that they can address their political blind spots; that they are interested in—and tolerant of—how others wish to live their lives but that they have their own way of dealing with that; that their talk of local control is not merely a ruse; and, crucially, that they do not believe that they have all of the answers to the world's problems. To their base, they must demonstrate that they are not hoping to backslide into the Bush years. The conservative hero worship of Ronald Reagan can at times be counterproductive, politically selective, and horribly repetitive—making it seem at times as if the GOP's plan for the future is to build a time machine that will take us all back to 1985. But, in attempting to work out what to do in what is a difficult and unsure hour, the Right might do well to return to at least *one* of Reagan's most famous statements: "The very heart and soul of conservatism is libertarianism." And without it, the Right is nothing.

2

WHAT IS A

"CONSERVATARIAN"?

———

THE term "conservatarian" first appeared on my radar toward the end of 2006, having been adopted by disgruntled Republicans who objected strenuously to the direction in which their party had been pulled under George W. Bush and, in consequence, aspired to distinguish themselves from the establishment. "When I am around conservatives," discontents would tell me, "I feel like a libertarian; but when I'm around libertarians I feel like a conservative." Sometimes they would describe themselves as a "liberservative" or a "libertarian *and* a conservative," or any other hastily assembled portmanteau that got the message across. Whatever the term, their meaning was obvious: *I'm not one of those guys.*

An essay titled "Conscience of a Conservatarian," posted in 2007 to the Free Republic website, provides a glimpse into the minds of those members of the Right who were souring on the Republican Party and its treatment of the party's ideology. In it, the author laments that "the ink on the conservative label has been smudged by too much abuse of the term. . . . There are people who call themselves 'conservatives' these days," he adds, "who leave me scratching my head."

Among the people by whom the author claims to be vexed are "neoconservatives" and "compassionate conservatives," who have failed to "enthusiastically advocate less spending by government" and "libertarians" for their unacceptable positions on abortion, drugs, and immigration. A "conservatarian," he proposes, is neither a "neoconservative" nor a "libertarian," but instead "a mainstream conservative in the Goldwater/Reagan tradition who subscribes to the fiscal and modern federalist principles of the libertarian philosophy." At the end of his critique, he suggests as an afterthought that "perhaps 'modern federalist' is a better appellation for my way of thinking, but the federalist label leads to confusion." (It does indeed, and I will return to this later.) "It's so much easier," the author concludes with exasperation, just to say, "I'm a conservatarian."

This definition, of course, is just one of many. Ask one hundred self-identified "conservatarians" what they mean by the moniker, and you will get one hundred different answers. But what is interesting about this one in particular is its combination of palpable irritation with the status quo and its unwillingness to go fully toward the libertarian side. Primarily, the author feels *betrayed*. He feels as if his party has left him. He feels as if there is a gap between its rhetoric and its behavior. He feels, in other words, as if the word "conservative" has been taken away from him. Like Martin Luther, who intended not to depart from the Catholic Church but to purify it, our friend feels compelled to reclaim his precious philosophy under a new and worthy name.

It is this purifying and clarifying instinct, I'd venture, that spawned the Tea Party. Tea Partiers are driven by dissatisfaction with President Obama's overreach, to be sure. But this explanation isn't sufficient on its own. As with the ostensibly antithetical Occupy Wall Street movement, the fervor that created the Tea Party grew out of dissatisfaction with the Bush administration's decision to bail out the banks in the wake of the crash of 2008, and then with the Obama administration's evident intent to accelerate down that path. It ballooned in response to Obama's vast "stimulus" package, and it *exploded* during the debate over Obamacare. It was conservative, yes. But it was also refreshingly nonpartisan. As the pollster Scott Rasmussen observed at the time, the Tea Party was populated by people who were upset that "federal spending, deficits and taxes are too high, and [who thought that] no one in Washington is listening to them. . . . That latter point," Rasmussen counseled, "is really, really important."

As often as not, the targets of Tea Party ire are on the Right. And nobody is safe: not former favorite Marco Rubio, not Senate majority leader Mitch McConnell, not House speaker John Boehner or his once-apparent heir Eric Cantor. This is simultaneously a blessing and a curse—a source of renewal but also of wasted energy. To borrow a religious analogy, one might say that the Tea Party exhibits the best and the worst of the Protestant tradition. The most beautiful thing about Protestantism is that any disgruntled Tom, Dick, or Harry can start their own church and claim to represent the truth. Likewise, the ugliest thing about Protestantism is that any disgruntled Tom, Dick, or Harry can start their own church and claim to represent the truth. In its early years, the Tea Party largely trained its fire on the Left and on what it perceived to be a conservative "establishment" that had let it down. Now there are strains within the movement that seem to be engaged in a perpetual game of one-upmanship, and for whom purity is regarded as being of greater value than is tangible success. On occasion, there has been something of Occupy Wall Street about the Right's insurgency—a tendency, that is, toward nihilism and suicide, and, most regrettably of all, toward the belief that martyrdom is the greatest of political attributes. At its best, the Tea Party is independent-minded, reflective of the grass roots, and ruthlessly effective; at its worst it is petty, superficial, and fatalistic.

At its heart, however, it is admirably honest. Tea Party conservatives are as likely as anyone else to express dissatisfaction with George W. Bush, with the growth of government spending during the first decade of the twenty-first century, with the wars in Iraq and Afghanistan, and with the housing bubble and the bailouts that followed it. The election of a Democratic president, a Democratic Senate, and a Democratic House raised hackles, and Barack Obama's open progressivism fueled justified fears that things were getting inexorably worse. These were the proximate causes that triggered the explosion. But the long-term causes had been percolating for a while, and they have not been forgotten.

This matters because, counterintuitive as it might seem, it is possible that the past five years of American political debate have been primarily defined not by Barack Obama but by George W. Bush. Obama ran twice for election as the anti-Bush, and to an extent he still sees himself in this way. When he says "We are not going back"—and he says this an awful lot—this is what he means: back to Bush and, by implication, to the war spending and to the economics that many Americans still blame for the housing crisis and for the Great Recession. President Obama may have failed to bring about an ideological realignment, but he has rather successfully managed to convince Americans of what they do *not* want. And in politics, that can be extremely powerful.

It is not just the center and the Left that have positioned themselves in relation to the last president. Republicans, too, have been scrambling away from the Bush years as fast as they can. When was the last time you heard an aspiring conservative politician say "As George Bush said . . ." or "I'm a George W. Bush conservative"? When was the last time you heard nostalgia for 2005? The mere thought is preposterous. This is not simply because Bush's name has long ceased to be an electoral asset with the independent voters who decide American elections, but also because the Bush years have come to be regarded as a long-term disappointment for the Right. Conservatives will effusively praise Bush for his leadership after 9/11. And I daresay that most of them, if pushed, would rather that he were in charge now than Barack Obama. But that's about it. On spending, health care, education, the role of government, foreign policy, federalism, and even gun rights, Bush's model is out of fashion. And, in spite of much soul-searching in the years since 2008, conservatives have yet to find a new banner under which they can unite. This, in a nutshell, is the predicament in which the movement finds itself today.

THE PERILS OF LANGUAGE

Before we go on, it's probably worth considering some of the language here. For disgruntled figures to cram the words "conservative" and "libertarian" into one term is certainly cute. In my experience, many on the American Right do indeed spend their time flitting between those two extremes—and for good reason: Both libertarianism and conservatism are seductive to the man who is motivated by a desire for ordered liberty. And yet the marriage also presents us with a real challenge—namely, that while conservatism and libertarianism share many of the same qualities, they are absolutely not the same thing, and, at times, they come into conflict.

The primary weakness of libertarianism is that it can become unreasonably ideological and unmoored from reality. At their very worst, libertarians can behave like Jacobins: disrespectful of tradition, convinced that logic-on-paper can answer all the important questions about the human experience, dismissive of history and cultural norms, possessed of a purifying instinct, and all too ready to pull down institutions that they fail to recognize are vital to the integrity of the society in which they wish to operate.

The primary weakness of conservatism is that, relying as it does on the Burkean presumption that society is the way it is for a reason, it can refuse too steadfastly to adapt to emerging social and economic realities and it is apt to transmute solutions that were the utilitarian product of a particular time into articles of high principle.

Because the two positions have in common a steadfast opposition to authoritarianism, these differences have tended to be pushed under the carpet when it has really mattered. But when the question is "What should we *do*?" rather than "What should we *oppose*?" they have come into harsh conflict.

Libertarians have a nasty tendency to start every discussion of policy with the pretense that both society and government are blank slates—which they are not—and, too, to pretend that one can apply libertarian solutions to a country and a government that is decidedly not libertarian—which one cannot. Libertarians can also fail to distinguish between the importance of a codified framework of negative rights that ensure free action and the manner in which those rights are used. The most salient criticism of the libertarian instinct—and I include my own tendencies in this critique—is that its adherents can reflexively defend *anything* that is said or done purely on the basis that it represents a free choice, regardless of whether or not it is a *good* choice. Thus do libertarians often ignore that crucial component of civil society: judgment. Just because something is legal does not mean that it is virtuous.

Conservatives, meanwhile, can infuriate libertarians by inconsistently applying the philosophy and rhetoric of individual freedom and by frequently becoming confused as to what the tenets of liberty mean in practice. As the *Washington Examiner*'s Tim Carney has been documenting for years, one substantial achievement of the Tea Party is that it has forced conservatives to recognize that there is a tangible and crucial difference between a government's being in favor of *free markets* and a government's being in favor of *big business*. Calvin Coolidge famously argued that "the business of America is business." This may well be so. But, insofar as it exists to interact with business at all, government exists only to create a stable environment within which businesses may live and die. It does not exist to privilege some over others or to ensure that existing corporations remain healthy and powerful.

Just as libertarians may underestimate the importance of what is being said and done by free actors, conservatives have of late tended to overestimate its importance, and thus often hold seriously contradictory judgments as to where the balance lies between individual rights and societal harms. A solid example of this is the thorny question of why most drugs are banned but alcohol is not. Conservatives generally fail to explain why this makes sense without resorting to the sort of sentimental, unpragmatic language they denounce on the Left. Since the resurgence of the conservative movement in the 1950s, there has always been a certain tension between the traditionalists and the libertarians, and therefore a good deal of criticism of a Republican Party that was tasked with synthesizing the two strands of thought. But in recent years, that critique has in some ways become deeper and more visceral— based less on a conviction that the party has ceased to serve effectively as a big tent, inclusive of everybody in the coalition, and more on a belief that it has flatly betrayed its soul.

In some regards, it has. As I established in the first chapter, the Republican Party has often failed to live up to its rhetoric—which matters, because an awful lot of people care about the issues the Republican Party claims to champion. As a rule of thumb: If your politics are defined primarily by an interest in liberty, you are a Republican; if you are more motivated by equality of opportunity than by equality of outcome, you are a Republican; if you want the state to be smaller and the basic structure of the American government to stay intact, you are a Republican; if you are interested in education reform, you are a Republican; if you are skeptical about the government's capacity to make significant changes to society, you are a Republican; if you think that man cannot be perfected, you are a Republican; increasingly, if you are pro-life, you are a Republican; if you are jealous of your religious liberties and your freedom of expression, you are a Republican; if you are protective of the right to bear arms, you are a Republican. And so on and so forth.

This is not, of course, to say that you have to be a member of the party, nor that you even have to like it. In fact, you may loathe it, as do many who nonetheless vote for it. But, unless the system changes radically, it remains the only realistic vehicle in town for the champions of a small state. A few holdouts notwithstanding, it should be clear by now that Americans who want the government to be bigger and more active are a lost cause to the Republican Party and the conservative movement—and that they should be let go. Republicans will never outspend, out-bribe, out-activist, out-divide, and out-promise the Democratic Party, and they should not aspire to. Instead, they should try to gather as many people as they possibly can behind their vision.

It is telling that "conservatarian" is the *mot du choix* and not, say, "Republicrat." There are a whole host of genuine independents in America—tens of millions, in fact. But my suspicion is that if you call yourself a "conservatarian," you are not among them. Instead, you are motivated by a desire to push the Republican Party in your direction, your choice being less whether to vote for the Republicans or the Democrats than whether to vote for the Republicans or the Libertarians—or, perhaps, whether to *vote at all*. Your worry, in other words, is not as to whether you are on the Right but as to whether the Right's coalition is constructed in a way that you find palatable. It is, after all, easy to be against things, but your wish is that those with whom you mostly agree would give you something concrete for which to go out and vote.

After banging around for a while trying to discover what he means, the author of the Free Republic essay finally settles on the term "federalist." This was no accident. It is, I think, becoming increasingly clear to some conservatives that the best way to run the country—and also to combine the various intellectual factions on which they rely—is not so much to "go libertarian" as it is fashionable to claim, but instead to advocate for a system in which as few decisions as possible are made from Washington, D.C.

If there is a conservatarian ideology, its primary tenet should be to render the American framework of government as free as possible and to decentralize power, returning the important fights to where they belong: with the people who are affected by their conclusions and who are therefore best equipped to resolve them. This way can many of the cracks between the libertarians and the conservatives be mended.

This way can the coalition's competing visions be best harmonized. And, most important of all, this way can the primary objective of the movement—to oppose the centralization of power and the establishment of a permanent ruling class that dictates to hundreds of millions from a faraway city—best and most permanently be achieved.

3

FEDERALISM

———

HERE is an important and instructive question: Within reason, does it matter to you how people who live tens, hundreds, or thousands of miles away choose to live their lives? If you call yourself a "conservative" or a "libertarian"—or, now, a "conservatarian"—I'd venture that the answer should be "No." If you routinely rail against Washington, D.C., and its excesses, I'd recommend that it should be "Hell, no!"

The Left and Right tend to answer this question differently because they have contrasting conceptions as to what constitutes the good life. The Left's dominant philosophy, progressivism, is built upon the core belief that an educated and well-staffed central authority can determine how citizens should live their lives. Progressives tend to be centralizers not so much because they lust after power for its own sake—although this is a human trait that needs to be watched, regardless of one's political views—but because they believe that they have generally applicable answers to problems of great complexity and because they need everyone on board in order for their concept of a fair society to work.

At its core, the progressive worry is that people who are left to their own devices will make poor majoritarian decisions—often at the expense of minority groups—and that the establishment of self-governing enclaves will lead inexorably to economic and social segregation. On matters of race, at least, this has significant historical—if not contemporary—justification. In other areas, it does not. Either way, the fear is pronounced, and it spills expansively into almost all areas. As anyone championing localism of any kind will know, to raise the possibility of returning power to the states is inevitably to be accused of channeling the architects of Jim Crow. In his less guarded moments, President Obama likes to make such a link himself.

On the rare occasions that progressives do cheer on local efforts at reform—as they have recently with marijuana decriminalization and gay marriage—their brief is not so much for diversity or local control *per se* as it is for the specific policies in question, which they hope will either spread from below to become accepted universally or be imposed nationally by fiat. Once they have reached a tipping point, with a majority of states or localities in their favor, the Left tends to regard political variation as an ill to be stamped out, not a virtue to be preserved for its own sake.

On Bill Maher's show in early 2013, I presented the case against expanding federal gun regulations, noting that New

York City was in need of different firearms laws than was, say, Utah. To me, this seemed patently obvious. There are 8 million people in New York City (more than in 40 of the 50 states), all of them living in close proximity to one another. Policemen can be found easily, and sirens can be heard at all hours of the day and night. Utah, on the other hand, is extremely large and extremely rural. Its population is just 2.85 million. A significant number of its people live at least half an hour away from a police station, which means that if Utahns find themselves in trouble—be it at the hand of criminals or of dangerous animals—they are pretty much on their own. Utah is also home to farmers, ranchers, and hunters. New York City, for obvious reasons, is not. Within constitutional bounds, surely there has to be some room for difference in the way New York City and Utah treat firearm regulations? (For that matter, there has to be some room for difference in the way that New York City and Buffalo, New York, treat firearm regulations.)

Maher thought not, asking how I could argue seriously that "all the gun laws should be by state" and suggesting that to believe that different parts of America needed different gun laws was as inherently "ridiculous" as believing that the residents of different states should (and could) operate under different health care regimes. South Carolina's governor, Nikki Haley, Maher told me, had claimed during the debate over Obamacare that the law was fine for New York but not for South Carolina. This, he thought, was absurd.

Unfortunately, the show ended before I had a chance to respond. But, had I been afforded the chance, I would have proposed that it was Haley—and not Maher—who was right.

The United States has at least fifty economies, and before Obamacare was implemented, there were significant variations in how health insurance was regulated. Not only does each state have different numbers of uninsured people, all with different health problems, but across the states there is a remarkably diverse range of *political* opinion, too. In the absence of a level of coercion that most Americans would find unpalatable, the acquiescence of the public—"the consent of the governed," as the Declaration of Independence puts it—is necessary for almost any political plan to work. *Of course* it matters where legislation is being imposed! It is no accident that Maher also believes that the majority of American states are holding the country back, and hopes that the central government will eventually prevail over the "rednecks" and bring everyone into line. He's a progressive. For him, political variation is a problem to be solved.

There is a good deal of snobbery involved here. Figures such as Maher often appear incapable not only of imagining that there is more than one way to live a good and happy life, but also of accepting that anything can be accomplished to a reasonable standard if it is not led by a cultural elite. Conservatives have long desired to abolish the federal Department of Education on the eminently sensible grounds that it allows unelected bureaucrats to impose their will upon teachers and communities who presumably know better what their students need than does anybody else. Bizarrely, the Left equates this plan with abolishing education *completely*. Likewise, when conservatives argue convincingly that the War on Poverty has been a failure, the Left concludes that the Right has no plan for the poor. When conservatives concede happily that they don't have a grand plan to fix all of the world's problems, the Left accuses them of lacking initiative, will, or imagination.

This is a brutal mistake, the result of an overdeveloped trust in the power of experts. In truth, their lack of a Unified Theory of How to Run Everything from the Center does not reveal that conservatives do not possess imaginations *per se*, but that they consider it safer for the country to be left in the hands of 10 million imaginations than just one. In his seminal essay "The Use of Knowledge in Society," the economist F. A. Hayek contended that decentralized economies would outperform centrally managed economies because they would leave local actors to make decisions in areas that they knew intimately, rather than requiring centralized actors to try to aggregate the sum of the national knowledge and make wide-ranging judgments for all. "The ultimate decisions," Hayek wrote,

> must be left to the people who are familiar with these circumstances, who know directly of the relevant changes and of the resources immediately available to meet them. We cannot expect that this problem will be solved by first communicating all this knowledge to a central board which, after integrating all knowledge, issues its orders.

This principle applies politically, too. Even when the central government proves incapable of living up to the promises of its cheerleaders, it never seems to cross their mind that its *structure* might be somewhat at fault. "It's not so much my personal management style or particular issues around White House organization" that were to blame for the Obamacare rollout disaster, President Obama told MSNBC's Chris Matthews in late 2013. "It actually has to do with what I referred to earlier, which is we have these big agencies, some of which are outdated, some of which are not designed properly."

Putting aside the obviously self-serving nature of this disavowal, Obama was actually hitting on something true: that the "big" and "outdated" agencies that have so much influence over our lives are not well equipped to deal with a country of 50 states, 316 million people, and a market that changes by the second. Most of them never were. Engineers know that the best systems are those that lack a "single point of failure"—in other words, that do not rely for their integrity upon a single, central system. Hospitals do not plug all of their life-support machines into the same socket. Why would the United States? More important, perhaps: If President Obama knows that the agencies he oversees are not designed properly, why isn't he moving to reform them? Why not acknowledge that the system is unwieldy? The clear answer is that he *can't*. His entire philosophy rests upon that system's power.

Honest progressives acknowledge this readily, conceding that their way of seeing things will inevitably involve some limitations on localism and liberty—and risk the occasional spectacular failure—but claiming that it is worth it overall. If you grant their premises, they are of course right. If you wish to fundamentally remake the national health care market, you really cannot allow the states and the people to try something different. Why? Well, because you *know* that your idea is better than theirs. Moreover, you cannot allow anybody to opt out, because you need to force the young and the healthy to buy health insurance in order to subsidize the old and the sick. And you cannot leave the system as it is, because that would mean that some inequality persists—and you believe you have the only way of alleviating the problem.

With a few glaring exceptions—the discussion of which forms a large part of this book—most conservatives and libertarians take the opposite approach: valuing the local over the national and the process over the outcome. Frankly, most people on the Right couldn't care less how others choose to arrange their finances or their homes or their communities. Providing that each polity respects the basic individual rights that are guaranteed to all Americans—and that participants are not physically violent toward those who do not want to be hurt—limited-government types have no real interest in the choices made by those in the neighboring town. You want to set up a Naked-Only Vegetarian Golf Colony? Knock yourself out, man. Just don't expect me to join—and if I ask, please let me leave.

This is because people on the Right are less interested in forcing outcomes than they are in protecting a framework within which individuals can live as they see fit. Just as to protect a man's free speech is not to tell him what he should say but to ensure that he will not be prosecuted for his utterances, to insist that most of the important decisions be made at the local level is not to tell local communities what their decisions must be but to ensure that they have the capacity to choose what suits them.

An honest appraisal of these two positions—federalism and progressivism—must recognize that they are utterly irreconcilable. To have a vision for how the whole country should look requires that you be intolerant of those who dissent; to care little how others run their lives is inevitably to allow others to opt out of your grand schemes. As the libertarian David Boaz has argued,

> *one difference between libertarianism and socialism is that a socialist society can't tolerate groups of people practicing freedom, but a libertarian society can comfortably allow people to choose voluntary socialism. If a group of people— even a very large group—wanted to purchase land and own it in common, they would be free to do so. The libertarian legal order would require only that no one be coerced into joining or giving up his property.*

This principle is not infinite, of course. In America, the existing "legal order" would also require that the citizenry be protected by those parts of the Constitution that the Supreme Court has applied to the states, and it would require, too, that the state and the local laws were obeyed. But that's about it. Should it choose to, the federal government could recede from our lives dramatically, to involve itself in only those few areas where nothing can be accomplished without a national policy.

That the self-appointed "smart set" would be tempted to sacrifice variation and freedom on the altar of promised progress was not lost on the Founders. "The first thing I have at heart is American liberty; the second thing is American union," wrote the anti-Federalist Patrick Henry in 1788. Henry was observing that expanded economic growth, increased exports, and scientific advancement—while nice and almost certainly the product of liberty—are not the purpose of the state's existence. "You are not to inquire how your trade may be increased, nor how you are to become a great and powerful people," he advised, "but how your liberties can be secured; for liberty ought to be the direct end of your government."

As far as is possible, conservatives should make this their theme, resisting the temptation to propose their own national schemes to replace those of their opponents and acknowledging frequently that the question of "how we should run things" can have a thousand different answers. Theirs should be a movement that recognizes that the best way to limit power and its abuses is to *fracture* that power, thereby bringing those abuses as close to the people they affect as is possible. Where there are genuinely national questions—immigration, the use of the military, the meaning of the Constitution—they should engage vehemently. Otherwise, they should decline to elevate every small question into a national referendum.

OUR FEDERALIST NATION

Variation is the key virtue of a thriving federal system and the most effective guardian of both toleration and diversity. Federalism allows the secular hipsters of Portland and the devout Baptists of the Bible Belt to live as they wish, providing a framework in which neither feels threatened by the other, and in which those who are unhappy with the culture of either place may move to more appropriate climes without losing the protections of their flag. Federalism allows Americans to say that if the residents of other states wish to smoke pot, "so be it"; if they want higher taxes, "so be it"; if they want to allow people to drink at 18, or to marry members of the same sex, or to carry loaded guns on their hips, or to drive at 75 miles per hour instead of 55, then "so be it."

This is a great thing in and of itself. But the benefits of this arrangement extend beyond facilitating choice and affording the aggrieved a chance to seek new pastures: it helps to prevent Americans from ushering in catastrophic mistakes. In *Democracy and Political Ignorance: Why Smaller Government Is Smarter*, George Mason University professor Ilya Somin argues that the combination of widespread ignorance about current affairs and the sheer size of the American state is undermining the idea of representative government itself. A government that is too big to master, and which is increasingly distant from the people it purports to serve, he writes, "undercuts democracy more than it furthers it."

This possibility had occurred to the more skeptical of the Constitution's authors. Worrying aloud that the federal government would eventually swallow up the states, George Mason asked his colleagues in Virginia,

> *Is it to be supposed that one National Government will suit so extensive a country, embracing so many climates, and containing inhabitants so very different in manners, habits, and customs? It is ascertained by history, that there never was a Government, over a very extensive country, without destroying the liberties of the people: History also, supported by the opinions of the best writers, shew us, that monarchy may suit a large territory, and despotic Governments over so extensive a country; but that popular*

Governments can only exist in small territories. Is there a single example, on the face of the earth, to support a contrary opinion?

The point is a crucial one. In the modern era, when we use the word "democracy" we are not so much referring to a system in which citizens exercise close control over their local authorities and reserve the rest of their decisions to themselves and to their families, as we are to one in which voters are expected to filter every decision and every public sentiment through the central government, more often than not sending their money to Washington, D.C., and then casting a hopeful ballot for the person who promises to return it in the most agreeable manner. This, in truth, is just too big a task for any individual to manage.

This is *not* because people are stupid, but because the federal state has grown too big and too complicated for anyone to master. Even if a person had both the time and the inclination to attempt to get a handle on the full implications of his or her vote, he or she would inevitably lack the information necessary to achieve the goal. People live busy lives, and they can generally focus on only a few major questions. (This, of course, is why the Obama campaign took to micro-targeting certain groups at the last election, telling women that Republicans wanted to take away their contraception and hoping that they would vote on that one issue alone, leaving the remainder of the questions to experts who knew better.)

In the *Washington Post*, George Will praised Somin's work, explaining that a salutary *ameliorative measure would be to reduce the risks of ig-norance by reducing government's consequences—its complexity, centralization and intrusiveness. In the 19th century, voters' information burdens were much lighter because important federal issues—the expansion of slav-ery, the disposition of public lands, tariffs, banking, infra-structure spending—were much fewer.*

Not only were they "fewer," but the American population as a whole was asked only to comment on those questions that were inherently *national*. The rest of the issues were de-cided locally—close to home and by those that they affected.

This arrangement yielded a number of advantages. Alexis de Tocqueville, that great observer of American life, wrote warmly of the townships of New England, which he regarded as both incubators and *generators* of democratic values. In the aptly named *Democracy in America*, Tocqueville discerned that the closeness of the people and their government served, first, to curb abuse, to establish a close link between the public will and the law, and to foster a responsiveness that cumbersome central authorities can never match, and, second, to demon-strate to those involved how societies *work*. Thus did the very process of the citizenry's being involved in the day-to-day running of a community teach them how to be good citizens. So effective was the system in breeding contempt toward top-down and distantly imposed authority that, by the time the British crown recognized that its neglect of its Atlantic empire was leading to routine insubordination and unprecedented in-dependence, it was too late: the people were hooked.

Within local communities, mistakes tend to be quickly

corrected and bad apples swiftly removed. Because law enforcement officers rely upon the goodwill of those they serve, they will quickly recognize a bad law at the point of enforcement. Likewise, if a town's people elect to spend all of the revenue raised from property taxes on, say, a giant chocolate cake, they will soon recognize the error of their ways. Why? Because the lights will go out and the streets will fall apart and their lives will become difficult. By contrast, if Washington makes a mistake, it can merely tuck it quietly into its giant folds and hope that nobody notices or cares—which, most of the time, having got what they want from Leviathan, they don't.

In July 2014, the *Washington Examiner*'s T. Becket Adams reported on a Gallup poll that showed "that Americans now have more confidence in the police and the military than they do in the three branches of the U.S. government." This, Adams concluded, "is not exactly a healthy place to be in a constitutional republic." Perhaps it is not. But it must be remembered that the federal government is not the only game in town, and its health and size should not be regarded as the sole indicator of America's political vitality. On the contrary: While the public's respect for Washington, D.C., continues to decline, faith in the states remains steady. "Ten years ago," the Pew Research Center discovered in 2012, "roughly two-thirds of Americans offered favorable assessments of all three levels of government: federal, state and local." Now, though,

> the favorable rating for the federal government has fallen to just 33%; nearly twice as many (62%) have an unfavorable view.

> *By contrast, ratings of state governments remain
> in positive territory, with 52% offering a favorable and
> 42% an unfavorable opinion of their state government.
> And local governments are viewed even more positively. By
> roughly two-to-one (61% to 31%) most Americans offer a
> favorable assessment of their local government.*

This admiration is not limited to those whose political philosophies tend toward localism. While there is a slight discrepancy between Republicans and everybody else, Americans as a whole seem increasingly to be more satisfied with their representation the closer it is to them. Just 20 percent of Republicans are happy with the federal government, while 62 percent like their state government and 65 percent like their local government. Democrats have almost identical views of the federal government and their state government (51 and 50 percent approval respectively), but like their local government the most, 66 percent of respondents rating it favorably. Independents, too, rank the institutions contingent upon their propinquity: the federal government gets 27 percent approval, their state government 49 percent, and their local apparatus 56 percent. Is this not a clear mandate for more local involvement?

The political pendulum has a role to play here. One of the reasons that Republicans were so dissatisfied with the federal government in 2014 was that it offered a Democratic president and a Democratic-led Senate. It is notable that when George W. Bush was in office, Democrats rated the federal government at 29 percent approval, while Republicans registered 53 percent satisfaction. But therein lies a key

point. The reason that the makeup of the federal government matters so much *is that it is so big*. Were its influence
reserved to a handful of important questions—as Ilya Somin
and his ilk would prefer—the integrity of the system would
not be so closely tied up with the transient political positions of its incumbents. That Americans despair when the
remote and unwieldy Leviathan falls into the hands of the
other team is instructive.

Partisanship goes only so far. As the *Washington Post*'s
Chris Cillizza noted in 2012, "most of the gap is explained by
the fact that people simply believe state government works
better." Specifically,

> *forty two percent said state government "addresses people's
> needs" while just 30 percent said the same of the federal
> government. Thirty six percent said that state govern-
> ments "can usually work together to get things done" while
> just one in five said the same of the federal government.*

It is customary for partisans to complain that the other
side is "obstructionist" or that it is "playing politics" and
"refusing to compromise." Just elect more of our side, the
typical pitch holds, and we will finally break the "gridlock."
This, I suspect, is bad advice. America being at present a
50/50 nation, the impasse is likely to remain well into the future, whatever the makeup of Congress. How would it be if,
instead of investing our hopes in a few Senate seats here and
a handful of Electoral College votes there, conservatives resolved to alleviate the deadlock by returning to an old but
simple idea: placing power with the people?

Respect for localism is, as much as anything else, a habit. When Herbert Croly, a founder of *The New Republic*, surveyed the American scene in 1909, he saw a polity that, in his successor Franklin Foer's words, "wasn't accustomed to thinking of itself as a national entity" and "certainly wasn't ready to be governed by one." Americans, Croly complained bitterly, regarded themselves as citizens primarily of their state and not their country. If America was to meet with his approval, it would have to abandon this conceit.

This critique was as bizarre then as it is now, for the system Croly was describing with such palpable irritation was not the product of a novel right-wing fever dream, contrived in a vacuum as a clever means of resisting the agenda of the Left and then sold dishonestly as an immutable tradition. It is *the entire premise of the United States's settlement.* "The federal government did not create the states," Ronald Reagan correctly reminded the audience in his first inaugural address, "the states created the federal government." The people about whom Croly was complaining were simply following the precepts of America's Constitution.

The country may have changed since the Founding— sometimes for good and sometimes for ill—but its basic structure is still intact, and that basic structure is federalist. America, remember, is a collection of semi-sovereign states— not of regional departments of the federal government. The federal government operates at the sufferance of a charter of limited powers that were selectively granted to ensure that those few things that the states cannot do on their own can be effectively achieved nationally. The states, by deliberate contrast, are where the real political power is supposed to lie.

This is why presidential elections are conducted through the Electoral College and not directly: because *each state* casts its vote for whom it wants to head up the federal executive branch. This is why, until the progressive movement pulled the wiring out of the Constitution and pushed through the Seventeenth Amendment, senators were elected by state legislatures: because the Senate was the states' representation in Washington. This, too, is why, until Franklin Delano Roosevelt's time, the federal government was able to intervene only in commerce that was literally between the states—and not to control anything that it happened to feel like controlling. It had its role, and the states theirs; it had its limited powers, the states more expansive control; the people looked to it to address questions of a genuinely national nature, and to the statehouses for everything else. However it might now be treated by politicians, the federal government was not created as a national repository to which authority would gradually be transferred, but as a body that would seek to do only those tasks that the states could not. Somewhere along the way, Americans forgot this.

The consequences of this lapse are manifold. We have now reached the point at which the majority of my fellow journalists seem to believe as a matter of faith that there is one—and only one—political office in the United States that serves as an indicator of public opinion: the presidency. Annoyingly, this conceit has trickled its way into our discourse. During the government shutdown of 2013, significant portions of both the American political class and the general public took reflexively to shouting "But Obama won the election!" whenever anyone suggested that another branch or level of government might have the right to exercise its own power. Likewise, whenever John Boehner announces a new project in the House of Representatives, he is met by a barrage of voices contending that if conservatives wish to make policy, they need to "win an election."

This makes little sense. Barack Obama did "win" twice, yes—and fairly so. But *so did everyone else who holds public office*. This includes all of the 435 people who returned to the House of Representatives—which is currently controlled by the Republican Party; all of the 100 senators in the Senate—which is currently controlled by the Republican Party; and all of the governors and legislatures in the 50 states, approximately three-fifths of which are Republican-led. To imply that one party or set of ideas is powerless because the president of the national government disagrees is, in the American context, absurd.

I suspect that there is a lot of political hay to be made by pointing this out. Each American, after all, has an issue that matters to him or her and an arena in which he or she would like to be left alone. Nobody likes having their voice drowned out by incessant talk of one man and his predilections. In consequence, conservatives should get into a habit not of targeting Americans with offers of government assistance or threats of federal coercion, but of making it clear to them that they are interested in creating a framework within which they might thrive on their own terms. This would involve returning powers to the states, abolishing many federal departments, and amending or repealing programs such as Medicare, Medicaid, Obamacare, and Common Core so that the states are put back in control. Conservative politicians might make it clear to all Americans that their personal views and their political views are discrete. They might, in other words, get used to saying "I don't mind what you do" when asked about issues that don't affect them.

The Right's pitch, then, could move toward being less against government *per se*, and more in favor of government at the local level. In other words, "Government is important, but if it is to work, it should be close to you." This approach, aside from being philosophically consistent, has other obvious political advantages. For a start, it prevents one from having to weigh in on each and every contentious issue. Don't like marijuana? Fair enough. Neither does Paul Ryan. But as a federal legislator, he also doesn't think it's any of his business. Not sure what the minimum wage should be in Ohio? Conflicted over the drinking age but unwilling to force the states' hands? Simple. Return the problem to the local level. This serves as a rejoinder against the Left's peculiar conviction that their aristarchs are all anarchists at heart. And it helps, too, to reconcile the competing claims of libertarians and conservatives, meshing libertarians' live-and-let-live attitudes with conservatives' respect for the nation's founding traditions. The Republican Party already thrives at the local level, with 30 state legislatures to the Democrats' 9 and 31 governors to the Democrats' 18. Why wouldn't it wish to return more power to its orbit?

WHERE REPUBLICANS WENT WRONG

The Republican Party is not hostile to federalism in theory. In fact, Republicans talk a good game, railing as a matter of course against Washington and praising the good sense and homespun wisdom of their audience. But in recent years, the party has often failed to practice what it has preached.

Take a look at the Bush presidency. While George W. Bush lived in the White House, his party controlled the Senate for four years and the House of Representatives for six. In those eight years, Republicans passed the Partial-Birth Abortion Ban Act and a federal takeover of education called No Child Left Behind, and the Bush administration authorized raids against patients who were using marijuana for medicinal reasons. As many of them do now, Republicans frequently called for a federal constitutional amendment against gay marriage—indeed, the 2004 Republican platform echoed President Bush's call for such a measure, arguing that "anything less than a Constitutional amendment, passed by the Congress and ratified by the states, is vulnerable to being overturned by activist judges." Meanwhile, apparently erstwhile defenders of federalism were happy to intervene in Florida to try to save the life of Terri Schiavo.

None of this is to imply that the Republican Party was *politically* wrong on these issues. Partial-birth abortion is a disgusting practice that ought to be outlawed around the world. But Republicans justified their ban by using the commerce clause—a justification they reject when Democrats invoke it on behalf of their hobbyhorses. Some educators liked the standard-based testing of No Child Left Behind. But it set a federal standard for education, thereby transferring something that is best handled at the local level to Washington, D.C. (In 1994, remember, the Republican party ran on a platform of abolishing the Department of Education *completely*.)

The War on Drugs, too, is predicated upon the virtuous desire to stop people from ruining their lives through addiction and to ensure that the basic principles of personal responsibility and accountability can be met by the greatest number. And yet it involves a deployment of federal power at which the party would balk in almost any other circumstance, opening the Right up to the reasonable accusation of hypocrisy.

Which is to say that the GOP isn't always wrong on the substance, but that it often violates its principles by adopting a *means* of advancing its agenda that it would lambast if the other side were doing it. It is true that most people don't maintain a principled position on federalism and then stick to that principle when it runs contrary to their preferences. Instead they just look to see which outcome they would like and go from there. But one doesn't create change by behaving hypocritically.

IF the Right is to have a chance at selling its vision to an electorate that, unlike that of Herbert Croly's era, has become accustomed to thinking nationally, it will have to answer a couple of potent charges. The first is that a more fragmented political system will inevitably lead to a broader range of outcomes, some of them unacceptable. The second is that, as American history somewhat tragically illustrates, some principles must be applied universally if the vulnerable or disliked among us are not to be cast aside.

As regards the first criticism, we should remember that the question before us is not "How can we ensure that nothing ever goes wrong in America?" but "Which of our competing variables should win out?" Regardless of what our friends on the Left may try to sell, there really is no such thing as utopia—nor is there a set of perfect answers that, with enough effort and care, can be divined and applied to all. All political opinions are the product of philosophical assumptions and the weighing of values. Do we prefer liberty or security? Do we cherish equality of outcome or of opportunity? How one answers these defines one's politics, the dispute being not between those who are ideological and those who are interested only in pragmatic solutions but between those who put different weight on different things. As the libertarian economist Thomas Sowell so pithily observed, "there are no solutions; there are only trade-offs."

A common criticism of localism is that it leads to unequal outcomes. Take education. While the issue is a complex one—there is so much more at play here than just money—it is reasonably well established that, on average, the worst school systems in the country are in the poorest states. In 2013, per the American Legislative Exchange Council, Louisiana, South Carolina, and West Virginia ranked last in the nation for educational achievement. The Bureau of Labor Statistics regards those states as being the eighth, ninth, and third poorest. It is not a hard-and-fast rule that applies to every situation, but to look down the educational rankings is to be left with the impression that poverty and low educational achievement are at the very least correlated.

For the sake of argument, let's assume for the moment that the two variables are closely related. Does this matter? Of *course* it does. But it is by no means the whole story.

For a start, there are a number of real and positive consequences of those schools being run locally, among them that the local politicians who are accountable for results can be elected and fired by the people affected by them (as we have seen in parents' fiery reaction against the Common Core curriculum), and that the absence of a national directive—or of federal funding that carries with it intrusive and prescriptive strings—creates space in which reformers might experiment without the risk of damaging the whole. Justice Louis Brandeis's observation that "a state may, if its citizens choose, serve as a laboratory; and try novel social and economic experiments without risk to the rest of the country" is crucial to the American ideal. It is this arrangement that allows reformers such as Louisiana's governor, Bobby Jindal, to test what happens when parents are given vouchers and invited to choose any school they wish rather than be herded into a catchment area; that affords Massachusetts the opportunity to rewrite its public school curriculum from scratch without having to worry about dragging down the other forty-nine; and that permits a state as diverse as California to institute different rules than a homogeneous state such as Vermont.

Do these virtues outweigh the potential downsides? In my view, they absolutely do. In the minds of many parents they do, too. But I would not pretend that they are perfect.

We see a similar dynamic at play with the provision of welfare. It is well established that permitting the states to set their own economic policies creates healthy competition, fosters innovation, and accords to the disgruntled the opportunity to move from living under one set of rules to living under another. As Michael Medved noted on the Daily Beast in 2011, the last census showed that

> *between 2009 and 2010 the five biggest losers in terms of "residents lost to other states" were all prominent redoubts of progressivism: California, New York, Illinois, Michigan, and New Jersey. Meanwhile, the five biggest winners in the relocation sweepstakes are all commonly identified as red states in which Republicans generally dominate local politics: Florida, Texas, North Carolina, Arizona, and Georgia. Expanding the review to a 10-year span, the biggest population gainers (in percentage terms) have been even more conservative than last year's winners: Nevada, Arizona, Utah, Idaho, and Texas, in that order.*

Were the federal government to more aggressively preempt the flexibility that these states enjoy—or to regulate the national economy to such an extent that states could only tinker around the edges—their success stories would not be possible.

Still, it is worth keeping in mind that not everybody can just up and move to happier climes and that, even if they could, they would not necessarily be better off for having done so. Since Barack Obama was sworn in as president, half of all the jobs created in the United States have been created in Texas. This is a remarkable achievement, and a resounding reward for that state's having consciously set itself up as a magnet for business and a refuge for progressivism's many discontents. Nonetheless, Texas also boasts the highest percentage of residents without health insurance in the country—not an advantage for those who have no realistic means of leaving the state. One can consider that economic dynamism and a limited safety net are related, as I do. One can contend that there are presumably many among that number who do not wish to purchase health insurance. One can note, too, that the health care systems set up to care for the poor are often worse than useless. But one cannot ignore that having such a large number of uninsured residents is a problem—the ugly downside, perhaps, to solid economic growth. Conservatives who wish to sell the manifold advantages of local control should be ready to concede such drawbacks, and to explain why they are outweighed overall.

The second criticism is perhaps a more straightforward one to address. "States' rights," once an innocuous term that described little more than the legal and philosophical presumption that the lion's share of the state's power would lie primarily at the local level, has become sadly synonymous with "racism" in the American lexicon. One can understand why. For years, recalcitrant Southern states justified vile institutions such as segregation and blocked legislation intended to outlaw lynching on the grounds that social and legal policy was theirs to set and that the federal government did not have the legal right to intrude. This is a position that was rightly rejected, and should be now, too. While it seems extraordinarily unlikely that the United States is destined to backslide into a Jim Crow regime—the relative racial harmony that Americans enjoy now is not the product of the scaffolding that civil rights measures erected, but of the strong and permanent changes that it helped to usher in—and while we could, I suspect, repeal a great deal of the legislation that once was necessary for keeping many parts of the country from targeting the vulnerable, there will always be new challenges and new pockets in which real problems will spring up. When making their case for local control, conservatives should be firm in their conviction that protections aimed at defending the fundamental rights of all Americans are best achieved at the national level and should not be at the mercy of local politics.

There is, after all, a significant difference between running a one-size-fits-all health care, pension, or education system from Washington, D.C., and codifying statutes that set basic rules and thereby ensure that the promise of the Declaration of Independence is fulfilled. As a general rule, the federal government should be in the business of ensuring that government services, if offered, are offered to all who are eligible. It should not necessarily be in the business of running those services. Explaining happily that there is a strong federal role to play in the maintenance of essential liberties, but that Washington cannot be expected to effectively play a role much greater than that of referee, is the defining conservative challenge of the twenty-first century. There is no going back to the days of Selma and Montgomery, but this has almost nothing to do with the question of whether a man in a suit a mile away from the Washington Monument should be determining the nature of the public school curriculum in Utah or the health, energy, and labor regulations that bind San Antonio, Texas. Ultimately, the instinct to fragment and return power is a liberating and an empowering one. It's time to make more use of it.

4

OUTSIDE THE GOVERNMENT

———

"POLITICS," Andrew Breitbart famously observed, "is downstream from culture." Is it any surprise that the Right is parched?

Over the last half-century or so, the professional Left has insinuated itself brilliantly into the nation's cultural life, securing a veritable death grip upon many of its most crucial and cherished institutions and affording a relatively small elite the opportunity to filter the politics of a wildly complex and eminently diverse nation through the prejudices of the two coasts. In the media, in the education system, and in our prevailing expectations of government, conservatives are at a palpable disadvantage before they even reach positions of power.

Come election time, Republicans are battling not merely Democrats but also the education system, the *New York Times*, Hollywood, allegedly disinterested presidential-debate moderators, a host of newspaper "fact-checkers," and the majority of outlets in the cable news archipelago, all of whom treat conservative ideas that are often well within the mainstream of American thought as if they were outré.

In a 2012 essay for *New York Magazine*, the progressive journalist Jonathan Chait conceded that one did not "have to be an especially devoted consumer of television to detect a pervasive, if not total, liberalism" in its offerings. "The work of popular culture," Chait added, "increasingly reflects a shared reality in which the Republican Party is either absent or anathema. . . . We liberals," he concluded, "owe not a small measure of our success to the propaganda campaign of a tiny, disproportionate cultural elite."

Chait's honesty on this point is refreshing. All too often, the beneficiaries of America's culture bias plead ignorance, pretending that conservatives have contrived the charge of bias from whole cloth and, in some cases at least, going so far as to propose that if there is a slant at all, it is a rightwards one. In addition to further destroying trust between the two sides, such feigned innocence tends to infuriate and to exasperate those of us who can see what is before our eyes. It is one thing for the Left to enjoy their advantage, conservatives gripe among themselves, but it is quite another for them to pretend that it does not exist.

Within the media, the numbers aren't even close. On every single measure—preferred presidential candidate, personal party affiliation, political self-description, campaign contributions—Democrats have the edge. Pick a year at random. 1981? Of the 240 major journalists whom S. Robert

Lichter and Stanley Rothman polled, 65 percent identified themselves as liberals and 17 percent as conservatives. Meanwhile, 81 percent of those asked had voted for the Democratic candidate in every election for the past 17 years. 2008? *Investor's Business Daily* reported that journalists' campaign donations went 11.5 to 1 in favor of Democratic candidates. 2001? The Kaiser Family Foundation discovered that media professionals were almost 7 times more likely to describe themselves as "Democrat" than "Republican." 2004? A Political Money-Line study revealed, according to the *New York Times*'s David Brooks, that "among journalists, there were 93 Kerry donors for every Bush donor." 2014? A study conducted by Indiana University discovered that only 7 percent of journalists considered themselves to be Republicans.

Academia is no less dominated by devotees of the Left. As Neil Gross of the University of British Columbia has demonstrated beyond any reasonable doubt, universities attract people of a leftward disposition. While conservatives "tend to cluster in fields like accounting, information management, marketing, and electrical engineering," Gross writes, those who identify as either "left" or "liberal" head for the ivory tower as if it were a magnet. This, Gross contends, is less because academics are intrinsically socialistic and more because academia is *seen* to be a bastion of progressivism and thus attracts those of a like mind. Left begets left, you might say.

As far as it goes, Gross's is a reasonable assessment of a complex situation. Still, it would be a mistake for observers to conclude that the domination that he describes developed *organically*—that is, that academia gradually and inadvertently reached a tipping point, beyond which it was pushed firmly into the "Left" column. *Au contraire*. While it can now rely for its recruitment needs on the solid foothold it has established, the Left did not wake up one morning and, as surprised as anybody else, find itself running America's faculties. It planned a takeover.

In 1962, forward-looking members of the radical group Students for a Democratic Society issued a statement in which they openly expressed their intention to "wrest control of the educational process from the administrative bureaucracy. . . . The University," they charged in a document that became known as the Port Huron Statement,

> *is located in a permanent position of social influence. Its educational function makes it indispensable and automatically makes it a crucial institution in the formation of social attitudes. . . . In an unbelievably complicated world it is the central institution for organizing, evaluating, and transmitting knowledge.*

Concluding its ambitious call to arms, the SDS invited its adherents and its sympathizers to "consciously build a base for their assault on the loci of power." Little did they realize just how effective their plan would be.

Tempting as it might be to ape the SDS and its remarkably effective frontal assault, conservatives will likely need to be more subtle if they are to reverse the Left's march through the institutions and to begin to shift the culture back in their favor. There are no magic bullets here. If the Right wishes to gain a foothold, it will have to do no less than construct worthwhile organizations of its own.

BUILDING ALTERNATIVE INSTITUTIONS

An old Irish joke tells the tale of a stranger who becomes lost on a rural road. Hiking to the nearest pub, he asks for directions. "Oh dear," a local tells him, "if I were you, I wouldn't start from here."

Like the lost Irishman, we have no choice as to where we start. Conservatives should accept this with alacrity and move forward anyway, recognizing that bringing about meaningful change will take considerable time and a great deal of concerted, expensive, and often discouraging effort. Whining, alas, will simply not cut it.

This exercise is already underway—probably to a greater extent than you might think. Twenty-five years ago, when the Right began to notice that it wasn't just losing the culture but that its failures were having a palpable effect on its political ambitions, there was no Fox News to act as a foil to the establishment. There was no talk radio to speak of. Glenn Beck had not yet demonstrated how efficiently technology could be harnessed to spread a message, nor had he revealed just how brittle the barriers to entry were in the information age.

Slowly but surely, by virtue of technological change and old-fashioned hard work, conservatives have inserted themselves into the conversation. In the grand scheme of things, the media still leans Left. But the media as it was is becoming less important, and its competitors are growing in influence. Indeed, in some sense, the American press is returning to its sectarian roots. Between the Revolution and the establishment of mass media in the first third of the twentieth century, news outlets were not only manifold but explicitly partisan.

Papers and pamphleteers took ideological positions and un-apologetically commissioned and published polemical works that celebrated or diminished the public figures of the day in language that we would now consider to be extraordinary. For a short while, this arrangement was pushed to the back seat, mass media allowing a few powerful gatekeepers to shape a national market, television networks and national newspapers eating up the lion's share of what had been a diffuse industry. The arrival of the Internet smashed this trend, threatening to return America's media to its polarized and tailored past.

For the Right, this has yielded some real success stories. Nowadays, radio is thoroughly dominated by conservative and libertarian personalities—to the extent that progressives would rather try to shut down Rush Limbaugh than compete with him. Fox News destroys every one of its competitors in the ratings (on an average day more people watch Fox than CNN, MSNBC, and HLN combined). Glenn Beck has built an empire that, were he a progressive, would have launched a thousand glossy think pieces and garnered him an endless supply of innovation awards. And, of course, the Web has broken the stranglehold of the elites, allowing anyone with a story and a talent to thrive and to profit. As Matt Drudge demonstrated when he broke the Lewinsky scandal, the days of relying upon gatekeepers are well and truly over. Who needs a printing press when you have a modem?

It is not all good news. The extensive cache of conserva-tive misinformation that is buzzing around the Web at any given moment can lend the movement an air of paranoia, arm-ing activists with abject and dangerous nonsense and turning off independents who do not identify with the sharper edges of right-wing rhetoric. Worse, the ease with which one can establish a media outlet is helping to politically balkanize a society that has been in part held together by shared experience. Once, a nation's people asked each other, "Where were you when the Beatles played *Ed Sullivan?*" Now they watch channels that cater to their prejudices and they receive much of their programming through on-demand services that sever the link between the media and real time. For those who like to customize their entertainment, this has been a godsend. For others who prefer to go with the flow, it has become overwhelming and alienating. Either way, it is indisputable that things have changed, and that change has provided a remarkable opportunity for those who sit outside the mainstream. Warts and all, the opening up of the news has been a boon to the Right. "Art," the socialist playwright Bertolt Brecht wrote, "is not a mirror to hold up to society, but a hammer with which to shape it." Let's keep building hammers.

Given the manifold successes that they have enjoyed in the media realm, there is no reason that conservatives should refrain from setting similar goals in the realm of education, too. Unfortunately, those who have thus far engaged with the question have tended to spend their energy in the wrong place—all too often conflating their objection to the *content* that is being taught on the nation's campuses with an objection to the academy *itself.* The result of this has been to furnish voters with the impression that to be on the Right is to be "anti-intellectual" or generally hostile to learning—a grave and costly mistake in a society that is still obsessed with credentials.

Instead of railing against education as a whole, conservatives should seek to alter it. Loudly and proudly, they should insist that learning is a wonderful and necessary thing, but that all education is not equal and it matters greatly *what one learns*. Specifically, they should vigorously make the case for teaching the greats and the classics—that's "old, dead white men" in the derisive parlance of the Left—and they should seek to expose what passes for scholarship on campus today for the useless, destructive, self-indulgent, and downright ugly nonsense that it is.

City Journal's Heather Mac Donald summed up the problem brilliantly in early 2014, lamenting in the *Wall Street Journal* that English students at UCLA, who had previously been required to "take one course in Chaucer, two in Shakespeare, and one in Milton," were now obligated "take a total of three courses in the following four areas: Gender, Race, Ethnicity, Disability and Sexuality Studies; Imperial, Transnational, and Postcolonial Studies; genre studies, interdisciplinary studies, and critical theory; or creative writing." ("Bullshit," to use less polite terminology.) "The characteristic academic traits of our time," Mac Donald argued, are "narcissism, an obsession with victimhood, and a relentless determination to reduce the stunning complexity of the past to the shallow categories of identity and class politics. Sitting atop an entire civilization of aesthetic wonders, the contemporary academic wants only to study oppression, preferably his or her own, defined reductively according to gonads and melanin."

Conservatives should counter this trend, celebrating and fighting for the richness of the thinkers and writers who have come before us and who have stood the harsh test of time. They should also celebrate individuals who choose to take a less academic path, and attempt to channel Americans who might otherwise waste their time at universities into more fruitful fields. This is a sensitive issue, but it has become patently obvious in recent years that academia is not for everyone, and that in a host of cases, pursuing a degree can be an extremely poor (and expensive) decision.

Even President Obama, that doyen of the preening college cult, has noticed the monster that the modern higher-education machine has created. Speaking at a General Electric gas engine plant in 2014, the president made the case that training for a manufacturing role would likely be more rewarding than studying an esoteric subject such as "art history." "Manufacturing jobs typically pay well," Obama noted. "We want to encourage more of them." This rare descent into honesty drew immediate fire from his base, and Obama backtracked instantly. "Now, there's nothing wrong with art history," he joked, nervously. "I love art history." Later, he made sure to "apologize for my off-the-cuff remarks," even going so far as to write to an art-history professor to atone for his "glib" comment.

It is clear why America's first hipster president would find himself unable to deliver a critique of liberal arts students. But conservatives, being hardier sorts, are under no such obligation to pull their punches. They should refrain from doing so, instead making it abundantly clear that choosing a trade—plumbing, electrical, carpentry, engineering—is a worthwhile and respectable path, and one that can set young people up for life.

All of which is to say that, acknowledging that the supply of progressive educators seems set to remain depressingly solid, conservatives should instead go after the demand. College is becoming an expensive business: Student debt has topped $1 trillion. Costs are skyrocketing—without any great improvement in quality or return. And yet, despite this, attending college is becoming *more*, not less, popular. More than ever, parents and taxpayers want to know that they are getting a bang for their buck, and students want to be reassured that their investment is going to yield something approximating a paying job. It is clear that reformers are not going to convert the hordes of tenured radicals to their cause. Why not put them out of business instead?

American popular culture simultaneously celebrates two ideas that are at odds with one another. The first: that one might rise from anywhere to be president or to reinvent the wheel. The second: that all of our children should rise through the public schools, attend college, and come out waving their certificates in the air as if they contained the cure for cancer.

We love our dropouts. We celebrate figures like Steve Jobs, Mark Zuckerberg, Walt Disney, Ralph Lauren, F. Scott Fitzgerald, and Mark Twain—all of whom either did not finish college or did not go in the first place—not merely for their commercial successes and contributions to the arts but because they bucked the system and made it big anyway. Whether it is John Wayne riding alone on his horse or Rosa Parks staying seated at the middle of the bus, America loves its iconoclasts in a way that most other nations do not. "I Did It My Way" does not have quite the same resonance in Japan.

At the same time, we have bought heavily into an educational model that is extraordinarily rigid, worshipping at the altar of official credentials to the extent that we have begun to ascribe class values to educational attainments and to determine people's future opportunities on the basis of whether or not they are in possession of the "correct" pieces of paper. We do not object if someone quits Harvard to found Dropbox, nor if they leave school at age thirteen to make millions in Hollywood. But, equally, we wouldn't want them working at our reception desks or in our public schools. A non-college-educated American has an ever-narrowing range of options. He is permitted to become a millionaire but not to work at the DMV. He can apply for an audition on *America's Got Talent*, but not for a role as a clerk in a Fortune 500 company. In most cases, it seems, those who choose a different path than the one decided by the elites may not apply for a job with either the government or a large corporation, and may not therefore avail themselves of the sort of on-the-job training that they need to get ahead. As I wrote in *National Review* recently, "acquiescence to the regime is the price of a place within it." Obey the rules, or pay forever.

This would be problematic enough if the university system were churning out brilliant minds and offering substantial value for the money. But the university system is *not* churning out brilliant minds and offering substantial value for the money. Instead, an alarming number of universities in the United States are now more likely to provide their customers with a cultural rite of passage than a regimen of didactic excellence. Do those customers know this? I have my doubts. In late 2011, I reported the amusing tendency of the good denizens of the Occupy Wall Street camps to tell me indignantly

that "they'd been to college!" as if that made the slightest difference to anything. In response, I suggested that there was
nothing on their diploma that entitled them to anything concrete. I posited that aspiring students might take a look at
the scores of unemployed graduates who had assembled in
America's public parks and in their parents' basements and,
perhaps, consider *not* "occupying education," and I suggested,
too, that in a number of cases, the dissidents' choice of degree
was not exactly conducive to gainful employment. ("Employ
me: I have a degree in basket weaving!") Perhaps, I offered in
conclusion, they might have elected to have done something
else? This proposal was met with blank stares—and worse.

But I was serious. Unless you're going to college because
you have an abstract interest in your subject or because you
wish to do something that requires vocational training, you
might think twice about the wisdom of your investment.
For some people, it will be the best decision they ever make.
For others, it will be a grand mistake. As Richard Vedder,
an emeritus professor of economics at Ohio University, has
recorded,

> *we are turning out vastly more college graduates than*
> *there are jobs in the relatively high-paying managerial,*
> *technical and professional occupations to which most col-*
> *lege graduates traditionally have gravitated. Do you really*
> *need a chemistry degree to make a good martini? Roughly*
> *one of three college graduates is in jobs the Labor De-*
> *partment says require less than a bachelor's degree. The*
> *comeback always is college graduates make vastly more*
> *than those with high-school diplomas. True. But that is*

*comparing apples and oranges. College graduates, on aver-
age, are smarter and more disciplined and dependable than
high-school graduates—so much of the reported earnings
differential has little to do with college learning.*

There is a more sinister side to all this, too: namely that
the expectation that everybody with a pulse must go to college carries with it the considerable risk that we will start
looking down our noses at those who do *not* attend. (Britain has gone a long way down this road already, I'm afraid.)
There is, of course, some real-world consolation in being
"only a plumber": thanks to so many of the potential plumb-
ers having left the field in pursuit of useless qualifications in
creative writing or Arthurian Feminism, one can now earn
silly amounts of money meeting the unchanged demand. But
money is not everything, and dividing society up this way
is unattractive and divisive. Americans should oppose it on
principle as being antithetical to their national ethos.

It's not just college. Taken as a whole, American public
education reeks of dysfunction and mismanagement. Head
Start, a program that purports to confer an early advantage
on poor children, is an ineffectual disaster. Despite having
been lavished with money and increasingly centralized, K–12
public education continues to yield perpetually disappointing
results. And, while America has some of the finest academic
institutions in the world, its system of higher education has
become bloated, arrogant, and aimless—increasingly expensive but decreasingly useful.

The fresh thinking on this issue is all on the Right. Stunted by its fetishization of learning, hobbled by the structural need to appease the teachers' unions, and intellectually restricted by a reflexive belief in the rule of national experts, the Democratic Party represents little more than a champion of the educational status quo. For years now, it has had but one idea: more money for schools! Nothing can dull it. Not even the sorry educational plight of African Americans—a key constituency, and one that progressives claim to represent. School choice, the best chance for poor black students since *Brown v. Board of Education* was decided in 1954, is almost universally opposed on the Left. The bubble in higher education, meanwhile, has elicited not a period of self-reflection but a federal takeover of student loans and, from the party's hard-Left flank, a proposal to make it even cheaper to borrow.

These are the wrong responses. A good chunk of the problem with American education is, if you will permit the metaphor, that it runs on the wrong software. At best, the program is outdated and buggy; at worst, it is no longer compatible with its operating system. When running through the structural challenges facing our schools, it is *de rigueur* for critics to charge that the essential arrangement is stuck in the nineteenth century. Undoubtedly this is true. For better or for worse, the basic model of K–12 schooling was designed for another era—one in which the majority of graduates would go on to work on farms or in factories; in which the information economy consisted of little more than the telephone and the printing press; and in which higher education was the plaything of the rich. But there is a little more to it than that. Our system is old and ill-equipped for our times, yes. Worse, though, it is built for another *culture*.

In the nineteenth century, Britain, Canada, and the United States became fascinated with Germany (then known as Prussia). Despite the remarkable success that classical liberalism had enjoyed (the British experienced unmatched international power and the United States was growing stronger by the day), elites on both sides of the Atlantic were drawn nevertheless to Bismarck. Admirers were enamored of the nation's scientific achievements, its efficient government, and its military technology. But in particular, they envied the educational regime.

The differences between the Prussian and Anglo-American traditions were marked. Where the British, colonial, and post-revolutionary American education systems had prioritized decentralization, tended toward instruction in the liberal arts, and put a premium on students being taught *how* rather than *what* to think, the Prussian-tinged reformers of the late nineteenth and early twentieth centuries typically advocated a system that took its inspiration from the factory. Out went local control, individual attention, diversity of thought, and a focus on the classics; in came mandated attendance, prescriptive testing for both teachers and students, a focus on basic literacy and numeracy at the expense of the abstract and the ancient, and, crucially, a centrally defined curriculum. As Glenn Harlan Reynolds explains in his timely book *The New School*, the "traditional public school" has little connection to the American schoolhouse of old, but instead

runs like a bell. Like machines in a factory, desks and stu-
dents are lined up in orderly rows. When shifts (classes)
change, the bell rings again, and students go on to the next
class. And within each class, the subjects are the same, the
assignments are the same, regardless of the character-
istics of individual students. . . . A teacher in a modern
industrial-era school was like a factory worker, performing
standardized operations on standardized parts.

That Prussian schools were arranged in this way was not a bug but a *feature*. King Frederick William I contrived his nation's system of government-led education not as a grand didactic exercise born out of untrammeled noblesse oblige, nor as a national means by which his subjects might improve themselves. It was instead a means of control. Recognizing the truth of the Jesuits' axiom that to educate the child is to mold the man, Frederick saw an opportunity to consolidate his power. Prussian schools would serve not as centers of enlightenment but as foundries, in which obedience could be instilled into an unruly citizenry and the leaders of the future could be forged in the shape of the ruling classes.

Evidently, the instinct was hereditary. Frederick's son, for some reason known now as "Frederick the Great," liked to boast that

the sovereign represents the state; he and his people form
but one body, which can only be happy as far as united by
concord. The prince is to the nation he governs what the
head is to the man; it is his duty to see, think, and act for

the whole community, that he may procure it every advantage of which it is capable.

Thus would the head determine what the body ate. After Prussian forces lost to the French at the battle of Jena in 1806, authorities determined that the problem was that the soldiers had been thinking too independently. Ostensibly in the name of avoiding another embarrassing military defeat, the private schools were abolished and the Ministry of the Interior took over their role. The state, henceforth, was firmly in control.

It is peculiar that this system made its way across the Atlantic and into the United States—not only because the underlying Prussian philosophy was so alien to nineteenth-century Americans but also because, as the literacy rates of the time reveal, there was no great crisis in American education that needed fixing. Edwin West, of *The Freeman*, points to a contribution in the January 1828 edition of the *American Journal of Education* that suggests that Americans enjoyed widespread literacy. By 1840, some measures indicate, more than 90 percent of Americans could read and write.

Still, adopt it Americans did. Horace Mann, an early educational reformer, returned from Prussia in 1843 deeply impressed by what he had seen. Using his power as the head of Massachusetts' first Board of Education, Mann ignored the eminently reasonable objections of his critics and pushed forward with his reforms, adopting the Prussian education system for all schools in his state. For Mann, the imposition of a statewide regime presented an opportunity to kill a few birds with one stone: In one fell swoop, the state could prepare

Americans for the coming wave of industrialization, ensure ideological conformity among a citizenry that was becoming more religiously diverse, and "equalize the conditions of men." Never mind that, according to NYU Professor Neil Postman, both Massachusetts and neighboring Connecticut enjoyed literacy rates of 95 percent for men and 62 percent for women as early 1640 and 1700; never mind that at the time that George Washington was being elected to a second presidential term, Massachusetts had a population that was more literate than it is today; never mind, even, that as Mann geared up to sell his reforms during the 1830s, Massachusetts boasted a literacy rate of 98 percent (today it is 91 percent). He wanted a change, and he was determined to get it.

By 1917 almost every state in the Union had followed Massachusetts' example. Indeed, so complete had been the Prussian takeover that Ellwood P. Cubberley, an influential progressive and the grandfather of a good deal of America's modern educational bureaucracy, wrote bluntly just after the First World War that America's schools "are, in a sense, factories in which the raw products (children) are to be shaped and fashioned into products to meet the various demands of life."

To get a handle on the scale of the cultural digression, we might ask how this ideal differs from the vision of, say, the founding generation. Superficially, at least, we observe references in their writings to the shaping of young minds. Consider, for example, the Prussian educational reformer Frans de Hovre's 1917 suggestion that

> *a fundamental feature of German education [is] education to the State, education for the State, education by the*

State. The Volksschule is a direct result of a national prin-
ciple aimed at national unity. The State is the supreme end
in view.

Compare this with Noah Webster's contention that the
role of the school was to "implant in the minds of the American youth the principles of virtue and of liberty and inspire
them with just and liberal ideas of government and with an
inviolable attachment to their own country," and to George
Washington's proposition that his countrymen "ought to
deprecate the hazard attending ardent and susceptible minds,
from being too strongly, and too early prepossessed in favor
of other political systems, before they are capable of appreci-
ating their own." Do all countries seek the same end?

Certainly, the ideal of universal education predates the
Anglo-American fascination with all things Teutonic. In 1817
a post-presidential Thomas Jefferson drafted a remarkably
ambitious educational system for his state of Virginia, the
purpose of which, he wrote, was to teach "all of the children
of the state" and thus to "diffuse knowledge more generally
through the mass of the people." For its day, it was little short
of radical. Abandoning pedagogic traditions that had gone
back to the beginning of time, Jefferson divided his preferred
system into three stages, detailing the ages at which students
would attend each type of school and which of them would
be permitted to progress; outlining what he considered to be
the best curriculum in order to ensure "the preservation of
freedom and happiness"; and even going so far as to suggest
that children who did not study would be prone to "insubordination" and to "premature ideas of independence," both of

which, he averred, were the "principle cause of decay since the Revolution."

Nevertheless, Jefferson recognized that such a scheme was open to considerable abuse. Specifically, he worried that the system could easily be taken over by the national or state government and set at a distance from those it was intended to serve; and that teachers with captive audiences could potentially use their positions to instruct the young in a manner that ran contrary to the principles of the new nation—or, worse, adopted the "manners, morals, and habits" of others. In consequence, Jefferson expressed his opposition to teachers being told what textbooks they had to use, was more than comfortable with professors being hired and dismissed on the basis of their political outlook (so worried was he that the academy might be captured by the wrong sort of people that he considered the teaching of federalism to be a fireable offense!), and even conceded his willingness to permit recalcitrant parents to opt out of the system. Most important, perhaps, Jefferson vigorously opposed centralization, writing caustically that "if it is believed that these elementary schools will be better managed by the governor and council, the commissioners of the literary fund, or any other general authority of the government, than by the parents within each ward, it is a belief against all experience."

That the educational power structure should be heavily fractured was a theme to which he would return time and time again. The "way to have good and safe government" of the schools, he wrote in 1816, "is not to trust it all to one, but to divide it among the many, distributing to every one exactly the functions he is competent to." The following year, he spelled this principle out even more clearly, writing that "It is surely better, then, to place each school at once under the care of those most interested in its conduct"—namely, parents, teachers, and the local community. If the system were to work as intended, Jefferson posited, it would need to be divided into "hundreds" of "wards." That way, abuses would be checked and remedied by the people who were being affected by them.

Which is to say that the *purpose* of Jefferson's system was diametrically opposed to that of Frederick the Great's. Like his contemporaries, Jefferson wished to see an educated population, and he was willing to tax the people in order to accommodate it. But he considered that individuals should educate themselves not in order to follow the dictates of the state, but in order to preserve among the people the qualities necessary for self-government. "For classical learning," he explained, "I have ever been a zealous advocate." Why? Because such an approach afforded a student the opportunity to "calculate for himself," to "express and preserve his ideas, his contracts and accounts," and to have instilled in him when young "the precious blessings of liberty." Writing to George Wythe in 1786, Jefferson urged "a crusade against ignorance"—not so that the state might be able to recruit the people to its side more efficiently, but because "the people alone can protect us against" the return of monarchy.

This was a widely held belief among his contemporaries. One year before the Revolution, Samuel Adams had predicted that "no people will tamely surrender their Liberties, nor can any be easily subdued, when knowledge is diffusd and Virtue is preservd." But, he argued, "when People are universally ignorant, and debauchd in their Manners, they will sink

under their own weight without the Aid of foreign Invaders."
George Washington concurred, writing in 1784 that "the best
means of forming a manly, virtuous, and happy people will
be found in the right education of youth." Evidently, there is
a crucial dissimilarity between an educational system that is
run from the center and one that is fractured and controlled
locally. Plain, too, is that preparing an individual to function
within and to understand the limited but essential framework
of a free system is a different thing altogether from preparing automatons who might fight battles more efficiently and
submit more readily to the appeal of "national unity." In
his *A Defence of the Constitutions of Government of the United
States of America*, John Adams put it well: "Children," he
wrote, "should be educated and instructed in the principles
of freedom."

So much for all that. Instead, America has ended up with
the worst possible system. Ours is a mechanism that is based
upon the design of a foreign culture, that has been wildly centralized, that is dominated by political ideas that are opposed
to the values of the nation, and that is prescriptive rather than
liberating. Most important, the combination of a large and active national government and an educational system that aims
to determine the content of the curriculum, that privileges
state-issued credentials above experience, and that still operates on the factory principle is an inevitably toxic one. If there
is to be a system of mandatory taxpayer-funded education,
conservatives might focus their efforts on making one more
like Thomas Jefferson's vision than Frederick the Great's.

* * *

AT this point, I can only presume that a significant number of readers are about ready to punch a hole through the wall in frustration and displeasure. I empathize, acknowledging fully that the prospect of waging permanent political, cultural, and educational campaigns is unlovely to those of a conservative disposition. "Activist" and "organizer" have long been words primarily associated with the Left, and for good reason: The politicized life is not something to which anyone should aspire, an ideal world being one in which the gap between civil society and politics is considerable and in which the private and the public are protected from one another by a sturdy wall of separation. But, whether they like it or not, conservatives are now living in a heavily politicized country, and if they wish to prevail, they need to understand that the fight has come to them, and they must begin to do something about it.

One tool they can use is the government itself—not, of course, by demonstrating to the public what it can do, but by showing what it should *not*. The rise of the president as a national figurehead and political celebrity of sorts has done considerable damage to traditional Republican notions of limited government and local variation, and presents a significant stumbling block to the aims of the modern Right. During the republic's formative years, the first vice president, John Adams, was keen to elevate the president's station to that of an elected king, lobbying hard for George Washington to be given the title of "His High Mightiness" or "His Mighty Benign Highness" or "His Majesty the President." Tired of honorifics, and having abolished all titles in the recently ratified Constitution, the more modest instincts of Adams's rivals won out. America's chief executive would simply be

Mr. President. (For his troubles, senators labeled the portly Adams "His Rotundity.")

Adams lost that battle, but one can't help but feel that his conception has prevailed in the long run. In the course of eighty years, America has gone from Calvin Coolidge to Barack Obama, undergoing an astonishing transformation of power and of expectation in which the Republican Party has, sadly, been heavily complicit.

In the 1920s, Calvin Coolidge was so determined not to undermine the nation's egalitarian ideals that he took to arguing with his housekeeper over the cost of steak dinners at the White House and to berating the executive branch he headed up for using too many pencils. A few years later, Eleanor Roosevelt sought to refuse Secret Service protection on the grounds that being surrounded by security would make her look "like a queen flagged by an imperial guard." One can only begin to guess at what Coolidge and Roosevelt would think of the situation now. The total cost of presidential transportation during George W. Bush's eight years in office was $2 billion. (Yes, that's with a *B*.) Each year, under Obama, the White House has billed the taxpayer for $1.4 billion in (nongovernmental) household costs alone. The First Lady's recent trip to Ireland cost $5 million—*for two days*. Call me a killjoy, but I would propose that it is difficult to make the case for a small government when the president takes a fleet of aircraft and a parade of armored cars with him on vacation.

It's not just the White House. By custom, we allow politicians to retain their titles for life. Throughout the 2012 election, Mitt Romney was referred to as "Governor Romney," when in fact he had not been in public office for six years.

One can only ask, "Why?" America being a nation of laws and not men, political power is not held in perpetuity, and there is supposed to be no permanent political class. Americans do not have rulers, they have employees—men and women who can be hired and fired at will and who remain subordinate both to the highest law in the land and to the popular will that it reifies. It is wholly proper for individuals to adopt titles when they have been hired by the people. But it is utterly preposterous for those individuals to retain those titles when their commission has come to an end. To my leveling tastes, even titles such as "Doctor" and "Professor" should be limited to the workplace. But at least those honorifics denote a permanent achievement or skill set. "Governor" is, by definition, a temporary responsibility. A citizen maintaining it after he has left office makes about as much sense as a retired CEO insisting that he be referred to as "Chief Executive" after he has left his post.

Gradually, many of the bad habits that marked the Old World have crept back into the United States. The State of the Union speech may have the air of a timeless tradition, but, in its modern incarnation at least, it is anything but. The Constitution requires only that the president "shall from time to time give to Congress information of the State of the Union and recommend to their consideration such measures as he shall judge necessary and expedient." It does not mandate that this information be delivered in person, let *alone* in a set-piece speech that has all the trappings of a monarch summoning her parliament.

Complaining that the president's going to Congress smacked too much of the British Speech from the Throne, in 1801 Thomas Jefferson strangled the practice in its crib, electing to submit a written report in its stead. This virtuous habit obtained until 1913, when, complaining that the presidency was not monarchical enough, Woodrow Wilson brought back the speech. For a while, the State of the Union became something of an ideological football. Calvin Coolidge and Herbert Hoover, limited-government Republicans who identified with Jefferson's concept of a citizen executive, gave their reports in writing; but alas, Hoover's successor, Franklin Roosevelt, insisted upon doing so in person. Since that time, no president has questioned the practice. The next time a Republican is in the White House, this should change.

So should many other unessential things the president does. Imagine the message that the next Republican president could send if he called a press conference and announced, from within the heart of government, that the state had grown too large and too expensive and that he would not be taking a $100 million vacation abroad that year. Imagine if the next Republican president made a public virtue of abolishing the State of the Union speech and explained in full why he was doing so. Imagine if the next Republican president openly refused to comment on questions that did not concern the executive branch. Imagine if, in direct contrast to Barack Obama's imperial style, the next Republican president frequently outlined what the White House could not and would not do on its own—in other words, if the most powerful man in the world took, in full view of the citizenry, to elucidating his enumerated role. Imagine, too, the conversation that would be started if Republicans began to insist that they were not to be called by their titles once out of office.

To an extent these suggestions are small and superficial, and in a country with this many problems, the failure of the president to be humble and restrained may not seem to be a particularly pressing problem. But they were not the most pressing questions in 1791 either, and yet in a time of almost perpetual crisis, the Founders took the initiative to explain and to demonstrate that a free nation requires certain cultural habits if it is to thrive. George Washington *chose* not to be a king, leaving after two terms by choice and setting an example that was eventually established in the law. Thomas Jefferson *chose* not to make an event of the State of the Union. None of the republic's early leaders gave in to temptation and sought to restore the crown—however perilous things became.

Conservatives would also do well to use the soapbox that their power and influence affords them to explain their philosophy to the public. Convenient as it is for those of us on the Right to imagine our opponents as a horde of power-hungry, amoral, devious Napoleons whose lust for authority necessitates that they suppress the ideas of those who don't agree with them, it is in fact the case that a remarkable number of the Left's leading lights simply do not understand what conservatives believe or why they believe it. In consequence, they mislead the public without troubling their consciences.

Jonathan Haidt, a professor of social psychology at New York University's Stern School of Business (and a self-acknowledged progressive), has examined the different ways in which people on the Left and Right see one another. To simplify what is a significant and impressive body of work, Haidt's essential thesis is that, for most people at least, politics is not a rational exercise constructed from scratch but the post-rationalized result of pre-existing subconscious assumptions.

Haidt identifies five values: care/harm, fairness, loyalty, authority, and sanctity. Self-described "progressives," he notes, place a high value on care/harm and fairness and largely disregard the rest. Self-described "conservatives," by contrast, value all five—although they define both care/harm and fairness in different ways. The upshot of this difference, Haidt suggests, is that conservatives are generally good at empathizing with the political opinions of their adversaries where progressives, on average, are not.

This makes sense. If, like the conservatives in Haidt's research, you believe that the priorities of progressives are valuable in and of themselves but that they do not represent the whole story, then you will likely consider the progressive worldview to be well intentioned but far too narrow. But if, like the progressives in Haidt's tests, you consider three out of five of the variables that conservatives hold dear to be morally worthless, you will consider your opponents to be charlatans who spurn what really matters in favor of useless ideals such as tradition and upright behavior. Or, as *The Volokh Conspiracy*'s Todd Zywicki puts it rather more bluntly, "many liberals really do believe that conservatives are heartless bastards."

Progressives are unlikely to change this view anytime soon. But there are huge swaths of voters in the middle who might—if, and only if, they are told calmly and clearly why conservatives take the positions that they do. As a rule, the Left fails to distinguish between one's view of the government's role in solving a particular issue and one's view of that particular issue *per se*. As a result, so do many voters.

Take the controversial HHS (Department of Health and Human Services) contraception mandate, which forces businesses, charities, and religious organizations to offer health plans that include contraception. Almost without exception, the objection to this from the Right is that (a) government has no role to play in determining the content of private health insurance plans and (b) there are serious questions as to whether the measure violates both the First Amendment and the 1993 Religious Freedom Restoration Act. The first objection, then, is of general principle; the second question is of specific legality.

Despite this, the Left wishes only to discuss the *merits* of contraception—in no way the important or relevant topic. MSNBC's Chris Hayes, an intelligent man, appears entirely incapable of grasping the matter at hand. In January 2014, Hayes suggested that the "issue in a nutshell" was that "one political coalition in America thinks birth control is a good thing, the other isn't so sure." Thus did Hayes presage the hysterical reaction that greeted the Supreme Court when it struck part of the mandate down on the eminently sensible grounds that it violated an existing law that had been passed to protect against such things.

Pace Hayes, consistent polling from Gallup shows that 87 percent of Republicans believe birth control is "morally acceptable," while a very slightly higher 90 percent of Democrats believe the same thing. Which is to say that there is almost no partisan gap on the question of contraception *per se* but that there *is* a divide on the question of whether government should force employers to include birth control within their health insurance offerings (56 to 36 in favor of the conservative position, as it happens). It is instructive, not to say a little worrying, that accomplished and intellectually capable people on the other side of the political divide cannot grasp this. It is heartening that, despite the ham-fisted way in which the Right has dealt with the question, the American people are still with them—and so, for now, is the Supreme Court.

The Left's rhetoric in this area neatly illustrates the core conservative criticism of the progressive Weltanschauung: To wit, that the other side sees politics, law, and principle as being mostly, if not completely, subordinate to their latest conception of what constitutes the good life, and that everything—freedom of conscience, settled law, established constitutional principle, and even a professed commitment to diversity and pluralism—is thrown violently out of the window if it gets in the way. As my colleague Kevin Williamson has put it pithily, "If there is one thing our 'social liberals' hate, it is liberty." Why? Because "in their view, you're free to do as *they* please."

Calmly and rationally, conservatives should highlight their opponents' inconsistencies whenever and wherever they can, and hammer home that their preference is to leave the question to the localities, to civil society, and to individuals—making sure always to frame their arguments in principled, philosophical, abstract terms, rather than taking the bait and discussing the merits and the details of whatever it is that is being imposed. "We have no issue with contraception, but we don't think that nuns should be forced to pay for it" is a winning line, and one that is difficult for a politician to argue against without sounding intolerant. "Contraception isn't that great" and "Why do you need the pill anyway, you slut?," conversely, are not attitudes likely to endear. Bobby Jindal—a man who is not known for his social liberalism—has proposed that the impasse might be resolved if the pill were sold over the counter without a prescription. Why haven't more critics of the mandate got on board with this plan?

Jindal's approach to this question is a generally promising one—a template, perhaps, for conservatives to follow, for their current political preferences notwithstanding, if the rising generation is full of committed collectivists, they have a funny way of showing it. For now, Millennials vote reliably for the champions of the New Deal. But in private they customize their lives and operate within bespoke networks of their own devising. This, ultimately, is a generation of nonconformists—one that is more comfortable with Uber than with the taxi commission; with Airbnb than with Hilton; and with Facebook than with Healthcare.gov. In a better world, conservatives would be their natural allies, defending the integrity of private institutions against the homogenizing Leviathan and playing Silicon Valley to the Left's DMV.

If they play their cards well, conservatives can begin to establish that the Left represents the man, the state, and the establishment—moderating and censoring the culture, and serving as the speech police, the arbiters of taste, and the purveyors of mandates. If they return to their localizing and radical roots, the Right can reverse a trend that has seen those for whom "liberty" should be a natural instinct fall readily into the hands of the progressives and come to regard "conservatives" as hypocrites at best and their enemies at worst. Gays, immigrants, pot smokers, free-speakers, dropouts, rebels, the politically incorrect—all of these people whose natural instinct and interest are toward diversity, small government, and local rule have been let down by a party and a movement that can, at times, be downright intolerant and rankly hypocritical. It will take some time, but if the Right can expand its tent, it can encompass more than both traditional conservatives and those who lean libertarian. It can encompass those whose labels are diverse and esoteric, and who march to a familiar tune: I did it my way.

5

WHY DO CONSERVATIVES GO ON ABOUT THE CONSTITUTION?

———

> To understand the fetishism of the Constitution, one would require the detachment of an anthropologist. Every tribe needs its totem and its fetish, and the Constitution is ours.
>
> **—Max Lerner,** 1937

IT'S THE LAW

Pace Max Lerner, there are no anthropologists needed here, for the importance of the Constitution is in no way difficult to comprehend. "The Constitution," Justice Antonin Scalia told students at Princeton University in 2010, "is not an organism. It's a legal text. . . . When you read Chaucer," he went on to propose, "you try to figure out what the words meant when they were put down on paper. It's the same thing with the law."

This simple idea—that the law is not only binding but that it should continue to mean what it meant when it was adopted—is a wholly uncontroversial idea in the United States, *except*, for some reason, when it relates to the Constitution. Then, we are told that the law must "grow" and "evolve"; that hard-and-fast rules must "adapt" to "changing times"; that the application of established standards is to be contingent upon circumstance and upon who is involved in the dispute; that words are malleable and sentiments fluid; and that the amendment process, which was put in place to accommodate and to codify evolving standards, is too complex to be respected.

It was not ever thus. A century or so ago, the vast majority of the people, representatives, and judges of the United States held the solemn belief that any significant changes to their national charter must necessarily be accomplished via the official channels—and *not* via the edicts of men in robes. In 1920, when it was decided that women should be added to the federal electoral rolls, the Supreme Court did not magically "find" female suffrage hidden within the Constitution's text; the people banded together and explicitly added it in. Likewise, when Americans (misguidedly) decided to ban the importation and sale of alcohol, they inserted a prohibition against such activities into the charter's body. The same approach was taken for the introduction of a federal income tax and the extension of the vote to former slaves. The alternative would have been unthinkable.

Nowadays, alas, making significant changes to the Constitution by way of the designated amendment process seems downright old-fashioned. Rights to sodomy, gay marriage, and legal abortion—none of which the Constitution addresses—have been "discovered" within the text. We are told that capital punishment, specifically referenced within the Fifth Amendment, was intended to be outlawed by the Eighth. And, since Franklin Roosevelt sought to fundamentally transform the country in the 1930s and threatened to destroy the integrity of the court if it stood in his way, the Commerce Clause has been transmuted into a General Permission Clause that has all but turned the federal government's enumerated powers into the police powers that the framers deliberately reserved to the states. If Congress sought to prohibit alcohol today, it wouldn't seek a Constitutional amendment. Instead, lawmakers would mutter something incoherent about "commerce" and claim the power to do as they pleased.

This is not, of course, to say that these developments are not in and of themselves good things—merely that there is a crucial difference between process and outcomes and that pretending that our highest law says what it clearly does not is a dangerous game. Contrary to the presumptions of the zeitgeist, "constitutional" and "unconstitutional" are not smart-sounding synonyms for "thing I like" and "thing I don't like." Instead, they are sober *legal* judgments, based upon a fixed text that derives its value only from its permanence. The United States being a nation of laws and not of men, our judiciary does not exist to make, to repeal, or to alter law, but to uphold it. Our judges are hired not to share their personal views with the people, nor to serve as a higher legislature that arbitrates the work of their elected representatives, but instead to referee the work of legislators neutrally and objectively, and to step in if their rules contradict the Constitution's text. Our courts are not there to make political decisions. They are not there to decide "nice" outcomes. They are not there to "fix" the national framework for the modern era or to make "commonsense" judgments. They are not there to make the people happy, nor to ensure that the good guys win. They are there to apply the law—whatever it says and however it was written—and to do nothing more. "If the Constitution is law," Robert Bork argued in *The Tempting of America*, "then presumably its meaning, like that of all other law, is the meaning the lawmakers were understood to have intended." And if it is not "law" but a living organism to be updated with the times? Well, then it is useless.

Think about it like this: If our judges are not making their decisions by closely examining the original intent of the law and applying it to the cases before them, then what *are* they doing? There are only two options. Either they are examining their own views and exporting them to the public at large, or they are attempting to divine the sentiment of the majority of the people. But if we are to have a Constitution that reflects the views of a majority, then why have one at all? We already have Congress to do that. And if we are to have a Constitution that is constantly amended by a few wise men, then shouldn't those men be elected politicians rather than appointed lawyers? The security of the American arrangement is that the Constitution sits above the will of the experts and above the transient views of the majority. If it is merely to be the tool of both, why not move to the British system, in which the legislature is sovereign?

Justice Scalia, a leading critic of the "living constitution" theory, expanded upon this point in a 2005 speech at the Woodrow Wilson International Center for Scholars:

> *If . . . we're picking people to draw out of their own conscience and experience a new constitution with all sorts of new values to govern our society, then we should not look principally for good lawyers. We should look principally for people who agree with us, the majority, as to whether there ought to be this right, that right and the other right. We want to pick people that would write the new constitution that we would want.*

Scalia was highlighting the absurdity inherent in the idea of "living constitutionalism"—mocking the approach as if it were fringe and unthinkable. But what he correctly regards as an intolerable usurpation is in fact *precisely how the Left tends to think.*

This is why, instead of discussing the legal acumen of nominees, we are treated to endless conversations about what judges *believe*, about *who* they are, and about *how* they see the world outside of the courtroom. Explaining in 2009 what criteria he would be using to pick his first new Supreme Court justice, President Obama promised to look for a "quality of empathy, of understanding and identifying with people's hopes and struggles." In a judge, Obama contended, each of these serves as "an essential ingredient for arriving at just decisions and outcomes."

This was no slip of the tongue, nor temporary illness. In 2007, before he won the election, Obama confirmed that he wanted on the bench "people who have life experience, and [who] understand what it means to be on the outside, what it means to have the system not work for them." In the same year, during a meeting with Planned Parenthood, Obama argued that America's judges should have "the empathy to understand what it's like to be poor or African-American or gay or disabled or old."

Sure enough, when the opportunity presented itself, Obama chose for the court a woman who believes that one's personal background is crucial to one's quality as a judge. Sonia Sotomayor, Obama's first nominee, famously explained that "a wise Latina woman with the richness of her experiences would more often than not reach a better conclusion than a white male who hasn't lived that life."

Empathy, life experience, and understanding are certainly all virtues . . . at least, in a social worker or a novelist or a politician. But they have next to nothing to do with the *law*. There is a good reason Lady Justice wears a blindfold and boasts a set of scales in her hand, and that is that she's not interested in what you look like, what you've been through, or where you're from. Just as it would be patently absurd for a judge in a criminal trial to sum up by making reference to the nature of the victim, so it is for the people we trust to administer the highest law in the land. Our judges take an oath in which they "solemnly swear" that they "will administer justice without respect to persons, and do equal right to the poor and to the rich." They do *not* take an oath to improve living conditions or to make outsiders feel welcome or to impart their particular wisdom. These are fine enough goals in themselves. But they are at best a distraction from—and at worst an impediment to—the duties of a Supreme Court justice.

Long before the pernicious idea of the "living constitution" had made its way into mainstream progressive thought, the Founders recognized the danger posed by judges who wandered away from applying the text as it was originally understood. Writing to Justice William Johnson in 1823, Thomas Jefferson urged that he and his countrymen,

> *on every question of construction, carry ourselves back to a time when the Constitution was adopted, recollect the spirit manifested in the debates, and instead of trying what meaning can be squeezed out of the text, or invented against it, conform to the probable one in which it was passed.*

Jefferson was by no means alone in his aspirations. In his farewell address, George Washington recognized that once the judicial branch started to ignore the law in favor of preferable outcomes, the Constitution would become meaningless. Washington recommended that

> *if, in the opinion of the people, the distribution or the modification of the constitutional powers be in any particular wrong, let it be corrected by an amendment in the way which the Constitution designates. Let there be no change by usurpation; for though this in one instance may be the instrument of good, it is the customary weapon by which free governments are destroyed.*

James Madison, too, warned in an 1824 letter to Henry Lee that there was great danger in any interpretation of the document that did not look back to discover original intent. Presaging the "emanations and penumbras" that would later be used to bend the document to the will of the court, Madison recognized that, taken outside of their intended meaning, words can be deceptive. "I entirely concur," Madison wrote,

> in the propriety of resorting to the sense in which the Constitution was accepted and ratified by the nation. In that sense alone it is the legitimate Constitution. And if that be not the guide in expounding it, there can be no security for a consistent and stable, more than for a faithful exercise of its powers. If the meaning of the text be sought in the changeable meaning of the words composing it, it is evident that the shape and attributes of the Government must partake of the changes to which the words and phrases of all living languages are constantly subject. What a metamorphosis would be produced in the code of law if all its ancient phraseology were to be taken in its modern sense.

Among the "ancient phraseology" that those who wish to undermine and circumvent the document's plain meaning have chosen to take "in its modern sense" are "general welfare," which is a meaningless piece of scene-setting pabulum that most definitely does not mean "welfare" in the sense that we use today; "necessary and proper," which was intended to bolster the charter's limitations rather than to augment its scope; and "well regulated," which has nothing whatsoever to do with government control of firearms.

If one is to avoid missteps like these and demand that the text of the Constitution be applied as written, one has little choice but to be preoccupied with the founding generation and with the culture and society that informed their work. Just as a scholar of Shakespeare must understand the Elizabethan era, anyone who believes in the American rule of law must inevitably acquaint himself with the late eighteenth century—with the prevailing ideologies, the linguistic norms, the political fights, the hopes and the fears of its leading players, and the circumstances that impelled them to write down some ground rules in the first place. As we will see, not everyone is keen to undertake that work.

OLD IS NEW AND NEW IS OLD

"When the Constitution was framed," Woodrow Wilson griped in 1908, "there were no railways, there was no telegraph, there was no telephone."

If one wished to help Wilson out, one could add a few more bones to his critique: When the revolution of 1776 began, we might record, Charles Darwin had not yet written his theory of evolution, electricity would not be harnessed and distributed for another century, and the life expectancy of an average American was thirty-five. Germ theory had not yet been properly understood. Nobody had heard of DNA. The microwave and pasteurized milk were distant pleasures.

Television, even in its most basic form, was a pipe dream. Man hadn't been to the moon. There was no baseball, and flight was reserved to the birds. You get the picture: it was a dramatically different time.

Whether this matters depends on what you think a constitution is for, and by extension, what a *government* is for. In the view of the Founders, government existed to secure the rights of man and to perform those few tasks that the people had agreed to delegate to it. Liberty was the goal of the state, and that state was expected to remain strictly within its guidelines. As both the *Federalist Papers* and the *Anti-Federalist Papers* make abundantly clear, the primary purpose of the Constitution was to create a framework that simultaneously checked and harnessed the ambition of the few men entrusted with power. Fragmented, not all-encompassing, power was the order of the day.

This philosophy pervaded the Constitutional Convention of 1787 and directly informed the charter that it produced. In the extent to which its political system disperses power and sets the branches of government against one another, America remains unique among the nations of the world. James Madison, commonly regarded as the document's "father," considered that "the accumulation of all powers, legislative, executive, and judiciary, in the same hands, whether of one, a few, or many, and whether hereditary, self-appointed, or elective, may justly be pronounced the very definition of tyranny." Notably, Madison carved out no exceptions for virtuous men, nor did he cast his work as being necessitated only in his own era. Writing in defense of the finished Constitution in 1788, Madison contended that "it may be a reflection on *human nature*, that such devices should be necessary to control the abuses of government." (Italics mine.) This conceit was uncontroversial among Madison's peers. Indeed, to the extent that opponents of the proposed Constitution believed his design to be inadequate, their worry was that the proposed checks and balances *were not strong enough*. To a man, the leading lights of the new country were agreed: Force was a responsibility best shared.

Today, when the Constitution's system of separation of powers is criticized, it is invariably from the other side—by those who believe that enough time has passed for a consolidation of power to be safe and that the American system, far from preventing tyranny, is acting now only to prevent the implementation of the brilliant ideas of the elites. Count, if you dare, how many times we have been told since 2010 that the House of Representatives' refusal to endorse the president's agenda constitutes "dysfunction" or "obstruction." Tally up the frequency with which it has been proclaimed that the minority party is holding the nation "hostage." Calculate the number of articles whose thesis holds that we should dismiss the Senate on the grounds that it gives too much influence to the smaller or less-populated states. Wonder, too, at the manner in which the president's frustrated supporters indignantly remind his critics that he "won" the election and should therefore be afforded a freer hand.

At the height of the government shutdown of 2013, a writer named Dylan Matthews took to the *Washington Post*'s *Wonkblog* to spit fire at the system and to blame it for having allowed the various branches to reach an impasse. Bitterly, Matthews complained that the shutdown was "James

Madison's fault"—the product of the "supremely misguided ideas" about separation of powers that had "made their way into" the Constitution, which document, Matthews charged, served as "an underlying disease in our democracy."

Specifically, Matthews took aim at the structure of the government, pushing back against Madison's claim that in order to maintain "control on the government," it was necessary to complement "dependence on the people" with "auxiliary precautions." Instead of our "potentially dangerous" arrangement, in which no branch of government has "formal supremacy over the others," Matthews alleged, the United States should opt for what can only reasonably be described as a democratic tyranny:

> *Max Weber, in conversation with Gen. Erich Ludendorff, advanced my personal favorite theory of democracy: "In a democracy the people choose a leader in whom they trust. Then the chosen leader says, 'Now shut up and obey me.'" People and party are then no longer free to interfere in his business. . . . Later the people can sit in judgment. If the leader has made mistakes—to the gallows with him!"*

In other words, President Obama should be able to do whatever he wants in his four years, and if the people don't like it, they can fire him. Minus the hangings, this is more or less how the British parliamentary system has come to work. In a 1976 BBC lecture, the British peer Lord Hailsham famously observed that the influence that the executive branch enjoys in the legislature has led to the creation of an "elective dictatorship"—precisely what Madison hoped to avoid in the United States and, inexplicably, what Matthews hopes to achieve.

Matthews's view is by no means new. In one form or another, ambitious progressives have been hostile toward America's rigid separation of powers for almost a century—complaining that it interferes with their grand vision, that it renders the state unwieldy and slow, and that it affords too much power to minorities who can use the levers that they have been accorded to prevent dramatic change. President Woodrow Wilson—who at least had the good manners to be forthright about his disdain for the system that he led—recognized early on that the Constitution was all but guaranteed to thwart his program for reform. And so it had to go.

"The Constitution," Wilson told a crowd at Princeton in 1904, "was not made to fit us like a straitjacket. In its elasticity lies its chief greatness." This, to put it as politely as possible, is veritable nonsense, and it says more about Wilson's own ambition than about the intentions of the men who assembled in Philadelphia. In fact, the Constitution was fashioned precisely to serve as a straitjacket—however brilliant and benevolent those it constrained were (or thought they were). The *whole purpose* of the American model is to play the branches of government off one another, slowing down action and assiduously preventing any one man or institution from accumulating too much power. That "inefficiency" about which the Left so often complains? It's not an unfortunate by-product of the settlement; it *is* the settlement.

So often what is really nothing short of a power grab is cast in the lofty language of "progress." Naturally Wilson was keen to assert that "the old political formulas do not fit the present problems; they read now like documents taken out of a forgotten age." But unless you believe that human nature has radically changed in the last two and half centuries, this should alarm you. When progressives argue that the Constitution belongs to another era, they are effectively contending that mankind has evolved beyond error and greed, and that the precautions taken by America's careful revolutionaries are no longer necessary. By contrast, conservatives who side with the detached wisdom of the founding generation are siding not with the antique but with the *perennial*. The men who painstakingly constructed the Constitution were extraordinarily well versed in the political histories of Europe and of classical antiquity, and were coming fresh off a fight with the British Empire. Harsh limiting tools such as a codified set of rules, the separation of powers, and the rule of law were deemed necessary then and they are necessary now, the primary objection to such mechanisms invariably being the good old-fashioned "but I want to."

A SHINING BEACON

On Bill Maher's show in May 2013, MSNBC's Joy Reid told me with irritation that I should consider neither the American Revolution nor the Constitution that it produced to be "great" because they failed to abolish slavery. "The revolution in the U.S. was 'great,'" Reid argued, her eyes flashing with disdain, "unless you were a slave, and then there was a war where 600,000 Americans had to die to make it better. Revolution isn't always great."

I explained that I thought that this was a "cheap" point, prompting Reid to ask:

You mean the revolution in the United States that produced a government that included enslaved Africans—it's a cheap shot to include that in the narrative? I mean, that is part of the narrative.

In one form or another, this is a common complaint. Reverence for the past is always a tricky thing, and invariably subject to one-sentence rebuttals: Admire Christopher Columbus? Ah, but what about his atrocities? Think Winston Churchill was a great man? Ah, but do you know what he wrote about Muslims? Impressed by Ancient Greece? But they didn't allow women to be citizens!

The conservative focus on the founding generation being a common and pronounced trait, the criticism should probably be answered. While Reid's distaste for my praise may have been especially sharp, she is by no means alone in pushing back against it. During the debate over Obamacare, the then–Speaker of the House of Representatives, Nancy Pelosi, famously asked a journalist who had questioned whether the proposed law would be consonant with the Constitution, "Are you serious?"

Reid is correct when she suggests that the sins of the founding generation are "part of the narrative." They should be neither whitewashed nor coated in sugar. But they are not the *whole* of that narrative, nor do they serve to cancel out its remarkable virtues. Any honest critique of the American Revolution must, I'd venture, do three things: First, it must compare the values that it established to those that were prevalent elsewhere at the time; second, it must take into account the *consequences* of those values; and third, it must evaluate their longevity. On all three counts, I consider the Founding to be a triumph.

The rebellion of 1776 did not *create* slavery, nor was it fought for the institution's preservation. It is a great tragedy that slavery was ended only after another seventy years and an almost inconceivably bloody war. But the unlovely reality at the time of the colonists' rebellion was that Africans continued to supply slaves to anyone who would buy them; the British, French, and Dutch empires continued to allow slavery both at home and abroad; and in various forms around much of the rest of the world, the practice continued unabated. As they swiftly discovered during the drafting processes, the architects of both the Declaration of Independence and the U.S. Constitution had a stark choice: Either they could have slavery and no new constitution or they could have slavery and a new constitution. Wisely, they chose the latter, failing to outlaw the practice but, as James Madison's notes make clear, establishing that a majority among them at least "thought it wrong to admit in the Constitution the idea that there could be property in men."

History is a complex and slow-moving creature, and rare indeed is the unsullied progress of Hollywood lore. The newly independent Americans did something astonishing with their rebellion—something that cannot and should not be dismissed lightly. In the course of a decade, they abolished monarchy, made illegal titles of nobility, and formed a republic in which the people were not only sovereign but could assert unalienable rights against a hard-limited state. They established equality as a national creed—if not yet as a national reality; entrenched and protected radical individual rights; and at the federal level, secured as sacred the principle of religious toleration. When George Washington came to the end of his military commission, the King of England asked the American painter Benjamin West what he predicted would happen next, prompting West to reply that he thought Washington would eschew his enormous popularity and ignore the calls for a dictatorship, and simply return to his farm. "If he does that," the King remarked, "he will be the greatest man in the world." Washington stepped down. It is difficult to overstate how extraordinary the new country was.

Ideas matter; good ideas doubly so. Evident in Reid's reading of the Constitution is the implication that the document represents merely an expedient set of rules for a new country and not a statement of timeless principles that would, by their design, eventually be applied to all. This is a misunderstanding. The genius of the founding generation's work was that it established a series of political doctrines that, like a shining beacon in the night, lit the way for the outcast and the downtrodden and gave vital ammunition to the weak. As Christopher Hitchens puts it in his criticism of Thomas Jefferson's final letter, "the American Revolution was founded on universal principles, and was thus emphatically for export."

Look at the major amendments to the Founders' Constitution: Do they revoke the original values of the charter, or do they expand access to them? Clearly, it is the latter. Textually, the basic liberties guaranteed in the Bill of Rights remain as they have ever been—untouched and unsullied by an amendment process that has been used remarkably sparingly. As it was in 1791, the federal government is prohibited from restricting the exercise of speech and the press, from preventing peaceable assembly, from refusing petitions of grievance, and from establishing a state church or interfering with religious exercise. It is not authorized to infringe upon the right to keep and bear arms. It may not quarter soldiers in private homes in peacetime at all, or in times of war without specific legislative approval. It may not violate individuals' privacy without a specific warrant to do so, and if it does so, it must establish probable cause.

It may not punish the citizenry without a trial or deny them representation, force the accused to testify against themselves, try an individual for the same crime twice, or take private land without compensation. It may not require excessive bail for those accused of a crime, nor submit the guilty to cruel and unusual punishment. And, most important but alas frequently forgotten, those living under the charter are to presume themselves to be at liberty unless it is otherwise stated. For those who believe in individual rights and strong checks against government power, there really is little to dislike.

The defect was a terrible but a temporary one, lying in neither permanent structural discrimination nor in ossified favor, but in the failure to share blessings. The founding generation instituted and codified great and beautiful values— revolutionary, timeless, imperative values—but they failed to ensure that everybody was covered. That is enough to mandate severe criticism. But it is not enough to throw out the whole kit and caboodle. Context is key.

It is telling that in the lowest moment in American

jurisprudential history, jurists bound by the Constitution's ironclad protections were able to exclude a class of people only by claiming that they were not people at all. In 1857's *Dred Scott v. Sandford*, the Supreme Court ruled that freed blacks could not become American citizens because, were they to be regarded as such, they'd start to behave, well, like American citizens. Such a decision, Justice Roger Taney wrote for the 6–2 majority,

> would give to persons of the negro race, who were recognized as citizens in any one State of the Union, the right to enter every other State whenever they pleased, singly or in companies, without pass or passport, and without obstruction, to sojourn there as long as they pleased, to go where they pleased at every hour of the day or night without molestation, unless they committed some violation of law for which a white man would be punished; and it would give them the full liberty of speech in public and in private upon all subjects upon which its own citizens might speak; to hold public meetings upon political affairs, and to keep and carry arms wherever they went.

In other words: Blacks would be Americans, with all that that identity entailed.

As if to leave no doubt as to what he was saying, Taney explicitly pushed back against the Jeffersonian ideal, writing that "it is too clear for dispute, that the enslaved African race were not intended to be included, and formed no part of the people who framed and adopted this declaration."

The decision was intolerable. But it was short-lived, and

since that time, the history of the United States has been a slow history of recompense—not of fixing fundamental problems with what remains a remarkable and relevant piece of work, but of augmenting access to its protections. The occasional mistakes of Congress and the indulgence of the Supreme Court to one side, the significant postbellum alterations to the American constitutional settlement have been *expansive*, not restrictive. The Thirteenth Amendment abolished slavery; the Fourteenth guaranteed former slaves citizenship and the equal protection of the laws and applied certain federal protections to the states; the Fifteenth ensured that American men could not be denied the right to vote "on account of race, color, or previous condition of servitude," and the Nineteenth that Americans could not be excluded from the polling booth "on account of sex"; the Twenty-Fourth prescribed that no poll taxes may be laid in the way of would-be voters; and the Twenty-Sixth lowered the voting age from twenty-one to eighteen. With the arguable exception of the swiftly repealed Eighteenth, there is not a single amendment that interferes with the original guarantees of individual liberty. This is remarkable.

Frederick Douglass, a freed slave who became one of the great abolitionist statesmen of the nineteenth century, considered the Declaration of Independence and the Constitution not his enemies but his greatest weapons. Sorrowfully aware that a good number of the revolutionary generation had themselves owned slaves, he conceded in a famous Fourth of July speech of 1852 that "the point from which I am compelled to view them is not, certainly, the most favorable." Nevertheless, he allowed, those men had "seized upon eternal principles, and set a glorious example in their defense." "With them," Douglass explained in a speech in Rochester, New York, "justice, liberty and humanity were '*final*'; not slavery and oppression." "Take the Constitution according to its plain reading," Douglass proposed, "and I defy the presentation of a single pro-slavery clause in it. Interpreted as it ought to be interpreted, the Constitution is a glorious liberty document." In the aftermath of the *Dred Scott* setback, Douglass felt not dejection but *confidence* in his conviction that the revolutionary values of the country's founding would eventually prevail. "My hopes," he wrote, "were never brighter than now."

Abraham Lincoln, as keenly aware as anybody of the contradictions under which the new country was struggling, expressed a similar sentiment in 1859—casting both the Declaration and the Constitution as timeless statements of truth that had yet to be fully implemented. Declining an invitation to speak at an event in Boston marking Thomas Jefferson's birthday, Lincoln sent a letter in his place. The present challenge, he concluded, was "to save the principles of Jefferson from total overthrow in this nation."

Those assumptions, Lincoln declared, "are the definitions and axioms of free society." And yet, to his dismay, they were being readily dismissed by slavery's obstinate advocates. "One dashingly calls them 'glittering generalities,'" he lamented, while "another bluntly calls them 'self evident lies'; and still others insidiously argue that they apply only to 'superior races.'"

Finishing his letter with a memorable passage, Lincoln proposed

*all honor to Jefferson—to the man who, in the concrete
pressure of a struggle for national independence by a single
people, had the coolness, forecast, and capacity to introduce
into a merely revolutionary document, an abstract truth,
applicable to all men and all times, and so to embalm it
there, that to-day, and in all coming days, it shall be a
rebuke and a stumbling-block to the very harbingers of re-
appearing tyranny and oppression.*

A century later, drawing eloquent attention to the persis-
tence of racial injustice in the United States, Martin Luther
King Jr. drew upon the very same ideals. Instead of agitating for an overthrow of the entire order, he instead alerted
his audience to the egregious inconsistencies that his generation continued to allow. "When the architects of our republic wrote the magnificent words of the Constitution and
the Declaration of Independence," King averred, "they were
signing a promissory note to which every American was to
fall heir. This note was a promise that all men, yes, black men
as well as white men, would be guaranteed the unalienable
rights of life, liberty, and the pursuit of happiness." Once
again, he urged, must the ideals be extended.

One can overstate the case. The hard-fought victories in
America's checkered history were won neither with parchment
nor with words, but with guns, with blood, and with unimaginable suffering. Slavery, like Nazism and other totalitarian
horrors, was vanquished by flying steel, by heartbreak, and by
brute force—by whites and blacks who together smashed the
institutions that had hijacked American liberty and perverted
it for their own profit. But triggers are ultimately pulled by

men, and successful campaigns require their practitioners to carry with them more than merely bombs and water. "Europe was created by history," Margaret Thatcher liked to say, but "America was created by philosophy." That philosophy, established by the founding generation and routinely recruited by the excluded ever since, remains extraordinarily potent—a North Star for wandering discontents within America's borders and without. "France was a land, England was a people, but America," F. Scott Fitzgerald wrote, "having about it still that quality of the idea, was harder to utter—it was the graves at Shiloh and the tired, drawn, nervous faces of its great men, and the country boys dying in the Argonne for a phrase that was empty before their bodies withered." To reject the giant leap forward that was the American Revolution would be akin to turning up one's nose at the Magna Carta because it did not immediately dismantle the feudal system or to dismissing the Allied victory in Germany because Eastern Europe remained unliberated from the Soviet Union. Conservatives rightly revere the shot heard round the world, and they recognize with pride its indispensable role in liberating man from the blunt force of monarchy.

They revere the founding generation, too. Not because they are old, but because their ideas were superb and their statesmanship judicious. The Founders were flawed, as all men are. But they left those who followed them with a remarkable tool kit, the likes of which we are unlikely to see again. To squander it would be an act of incomparable vandalism. Every generation considers itself to be smarter than the ones that went before, and every generation is wrong. Writing in *The Thing* in 1929, G. K. Chesterton observed that "in the matter of reforming things, as distinct from deforming them, there is one plain and simple principle. . . . There exists," Chesterton contended,

> in such a case a certain institution or law; let us say, for the sake of simplicity, a fence or gate erected across a road. The more modern type of reformer goes gaily up to it and says, "I don't see the use of this; let us clear it away." To which the more intelligent type of reformer will do well to answer: "If you don't see the use of it, I certainly won't let you clear it away. Go away and think. Then, when you can come back and tell me that you do see the use of it, I may allow you to destroy it."

Here, the role of the conservative is twofold. First, to act as that more intelligent type of reformer, standing in the road, chained to the fence, better to resist the incoming machinery. Second, to ensure that by the time the modern reformer has gone away to think about the fence, he has been subjected to such a protracted and thorough inquiry that he has come to his senses, conceived of its value, and renounced his intention to destroy it.

6

GUNS: A STUDY IN SUCCESS

SITTING in my room at Oxford in April 2007, I watched the horrible news unfold on my little portable television. A man had walked onto the campus at Virginia Tech and murdered thirty-two people.

This was my final year of university, and by now I had changed my opinion on firearms completely. Once I had exhibited the reflexive sneer of the British establishment; now I had arrived at the uncomfortable conclusion that the profusion of guns was not only uncontrollable in the United States, but that the attempt to limit their impact with flaccid and fanciful laws was also dangerous both to liberty and to the constitutional order. My undergraduate thesis, written that year on the passage of the Second Amendment, had served only to help me along.

It will come as little surprise to you, I would

imagine, that articulating this position on an English college campus didn't win me too many friends—particularly at a time when the news was full of death and grief. So, hoping to be spared the mawkish reactions of my friends—who, I figured, would probably come up to grill me on the subject as soon as they heard about it—I went and locked my door.

It didn't help. For as long as I live, I will never forget the look of astonishment and despair on the face of the BBC correspondent who had been sent to cover the massacre. Stopping to interview local residents, he almost immediately encountered a young man who suggested that, had more people on campus been armed, the carnage would likely have been stopped earlier. Another interlocutor urged caution, wondering aloud whether the state legislature's recent rejection of a concealed-carry bill had deprived some of the victims of a fighting chance.

This was almost too much for my fellow countryman to bear. A few miles away lay thirty-three bodies—still warm, and riddled with bullets—and yet he was having difficulty finding anyone who would tell him that harsh reform was needed. Spluttering and blinking, and trying as hard as he could to shake off everything he thought he knew, he made a valiant effort to grasp his interviewees' positions. But it was no good. For him, as with most Brits, the conviction that strict gun control is necessary is a standard part of the political catechism—absorbed as if by osmosis from a young age. Wrapping up his piece, he couldn't help but snidely conclude that the Americans' skepticism toward gun control was the product of an irrational and abstract belief system with which one simply cannot reason. I switched off the television, annoyed and worried. For those of us who believe in individual liberty, times of crisis are scary times indeed.

That America's gun laws are destructive and demented appears now to be the prevailing view among the establishment here, too. In the wake of the abomination at Sandy Hook Elementary School in 2012, we were told repeatedly—both by politicians in Washington and by a media whose coverage of the carnage bordered, frankly, on the pornographic—that the game was now up. "The culture of guns is beginning to go through a transformation in this country," the *McLaughlin Group*'s Eleanor Clift divined a few weeks after the bloodshed. Alaska senator Mark Begich, a conservative-leaning Democrat from a state with almost no gun laws at all, concurred, predicting a "sea change" in thinking. For its part, CBS News purported to have conducted a poll that showed Americans to be more upset and angry about Sandy Hook than they had been about 9/11. Pushed in a few cases by misleading questions and in most by the raw emotion of the hour, American attitudes shifted for a few weeks. And then, predictably, they reverted to their usual position.

And *more*. While President Obama rushed around like a headless chicken, trying to push through new rules before reason intruded upon agitation, millions of Americans rushed out to purchase weapons, to apply for concealed-carry permits, and to take gun classes. The AR-15, a type of rifle that was immediately vilified in the media and in Congress as being in some way responsible for the actions of a mentally unstable young man, flew off shelves like never before. Across the country, ammunition ran dry. Later we learned that the ten busiest weeks in the history of the NICS, the federal background-check system, were those following the abomination in Connecticut. Counterintuitively to some, a host of states actually *liberalized* their laws. Certainly the Democratic strongholds of New York, Connecticut, Maryland, and California all reacted in the way the Left wanted, banning specific types of weapons and introducing new obstacles to gun ownership. Amazingly, Colorado followed suit. But these states were vastly outnumbered by the more than twenty that loosened their rules.

Begich's "sea change," then, failed to materialize, the public coming to its senses before too much damage could be done. Indeed, even in those states that managed to pass new legislation, changes had to be made on the sly—by shutting down debate or invoking emergency measures that were designed not for standard legislation but for genuine crises. In many cases, the politicians responsible for reforms were met with sharp drops in their approval ratings—and, in a handful of instances, rewarded with early removal from office. In Colorado's first-ever recall election, two state senators—one the incumbent state senate president—were unseated by disgruntled and previously apolitical citizens for backing legislation that in most parts of the world would be considered exceedingly mild. Thus was reaffirmed in the second decade of the twenty-first century a lesson that President Bill Clinton had learned to his great discomfort twenty years earlier: If you want to survive in American politics, *leave the gun question alone*.

It wasn't always like this. When, in 1993, the Brady Act established a federal system of background checks and then the next year the Crime Bill banned the production, importation, and sale of a whole host of weapons, it looked as if the game was up for the right to keep and bear arms—that the regulations would keep on coming and that public opinion would move with them as it had in the other nations of the Anglosphere. In the 1990s, even former president *Ronald Reagan*—that great conservative hero—backed tough gun-control measures, writing in favor of the Brady legislation in the *New York Times* and describing as "absolutely necessary" the Clinton-era restrictions on "assault" weapons. But then something remarkable happened: Americans started to rebel, questioning the assumptions that had undergirded public policy throughout the 1970s, 1980s, and early 1990s. No sooner had Clinton signed his measures than the reversal had begun.

Gallup's polling team has tracked the change well. In 1991, a remarkable 40 percent of Americans signaled that they were open to a wholesale ban on handguns. By 2011, this number was just 26 percent. Similar reductions in support can be seen for a so-called assault weapons ban and for enacting "new laws." In 1991, 78 percent of Americans wanted "more strict" gun laws. By 2011, this was just 44 percent. Support for the regulation of gun sales follows the same pattern: In 1990, Gallup records, 78 percent of Americans agreed with the contention that "the laws covering the sale of firearms should be made more strict than they are now." Five years later, it was at 62 percent. A decade after, it was at 57. Today it stands at 49 percent, and it is still dropping.

In the early 1990s, pundits would have laughed openly at anybody who predicted in public that by the year 2013, all fifty of these United States would have concealed-carry regimes; that five states would have followed outlier Vermont in abolishing almost *all* of their gun laws; and that a unified Democratic government in Washington would in fact have *expanded*, rather than abridged, gun rights. Similarly mocked would have been anyone who believed that the Supreme Court would rule in the twenty-first century that the Second Amendment clearly represented an individual right and that the states were constitutionally obligated to respect it. "The natural progress of things," Thomas Jefferson wrote in a 1788 letter, "is for liberty to yield, and government to gain." Indeed it is. *But not here.* In fact, the right to keep and bear arms serves as a happy exception to the rule, representing a stunning victory for conservatives, for libertarians—and, really, for anybody who values reason over hysteria and facts over fear. The restoration and expansion of liberty that advocates have managed to achieve since 1987—at both the state and federal levels—is nothing short of remarkable, representing a salutary indication of just how effective the Right can be when it sticks to its principles, when it goes on the offensive, and when it presents a united front. Looking for the model for conservative reform? Study up on the gun-rights movement. Seriously.

WHY THE CHANGE?

When I run through this history for disinterested parties, they tend to ask, "Why?" The primary answer, I'm afraid, is a boring one: The anti-gun-control side has the facts on its side. Despite their protestations to the contrary, on a whole host of issues the self-professed members of the Left's "reality-based community" are anything *but* realistic. Rather, they are emotional, hyperbolic, and dishonest—and their positions are based upon claims that do not hold up to scrutiny and on a steadfast refusal to accept the United States as it is. Nowhere is this more true than on the issue of guns.

It is nigh on impossible to examine the issue of firearms in the United States and to come out on the side of the gun controllers. Gary Kleck, a professor of criminology at Florida State University with unimpeachable progressive credentials, should know. He tried. Kleck, who boasts memberships in the American Civil Liberties Union, Amnesty International, and Common Cause—and is a lifelong registered Democrat—set out in the early 1990s to write a definitive rebuttal to the libertarian-led anti-gun-control hypotheses that were becoming increasingly popular among rightward-leaning politicians and those among the electorate who were worried about crime. He failed. Working through the evidence, Kleck became at first concerned and then enchanted by the counterarguments, which he found, to his immense surprise, flatly contradicted the conventional wisdom. So he changed tack. Instead of producing his rejoinder, he wrote a book, *Point Blank: Guns and Violence in America*, which explained why, in a country such as the United States, gun control doesn't work. The positive and negative use of guns, Kleck concluded, cancel one another out, because "the problem of criminal gun violence is concentrated within a very small subset of gun owners." As such, gun control "aimed at the general population faces a serious needle-in-the-haystack problem." Translation: You can annoy the good guys with regulations as much as you like, but it won't solve the problem.

Kleck's volte-face made immediate waves. The American

Society of Criminology awarded him the Michael J. Hinde-lang Award. Marvin Wolfgang, a contemporary of Kleck's who described himself as "as strong a gun control advocate as can be found among the criminologists in this country" and conceded that if he had his druthers he would "eliminate all guns from the civilian population and maybe even from the police," was forced to acknowledge that his positions were simply not backed up by the data. Having established in no uncertain terms that he hated guns, which he termed "ugly, nasty instruments designed to kill people," Wolfgang wrote that Kleck's research "provided an almost clear cut case of methodologically sound research in support of something I have theoretically opposed for years."

Point Blank is a classic tale of fact outweighing fiction, of liberty trumping fear, and of the wisdom of the ages transcending the fashionable and the new. Until the late 1970s, Kleck noted, there was so little objective information on the issue of guns and violence that Americans were "free to believe whatever they liked about guns and gun control because there was no scientific evidence to interfere with the free play of personal bias." For decades, those personal biases were allowed free reign, first to inform government policy and then to ossify in the public imagination. The 1960s and 1970s were a time during which it became fashionable to pretend that society had moved past the need for timeless principles and could merely will itself into more peaceful and prosperous times. The combination of hubris and misinformation was lethal.

"Detached reflection cannot be demanded in the presence of an uplifted knife," Justice Oliver Wendell Holmes submitted in 1921. And yet for a time, it *was* demanded. By 1980, reams of new gun-control laws had been added to the books, while age-old legal principles that were contrived to protect citizens from predators had been either abolished or diminished (among them the Castle Doctrine and Stand Your Ground). For the Right, it was all going disastrously wrong.

But after a short period of quiet acquiescence, Americans began to notice the damage the measures were causing. Spiking crime, brazen miscarriages of justice, and a growing sense that the representatives of the people were catastrophically disconnected from the reality on the streets led to voters coming together and shouting, "Enough!" As researchers Steven Jansen and M. Elaine Nugent-Borakove have recorded, by 2001 an electoral majority had come to believe that the "due process rights of defendants overshadow[ed] the rights of victims"; that the state could not reliably help those in need of its protection; and, after the attacks of September 11, that their "diminished sense of public safety" was falling on deaf ears. They rebelled, demanding that their right to defend themselves be protected anew and rejecting the sloppy thinking that had marked that right's shameful dilution.

The Left, University of North Carolina professor Mike Adams argues, doesn't "like guns for the simple reason that guns—like prisons and military bases—are reminders of human imperfection." But, as we are reminded whenever we allow our politics to be driven by dreamers, man *is* imperfect. And history shows that good intentions do not inexorably lead to good results. By the time the new millennium was ushered in, Americans were fed up and hungry for new ideas.

Conservatives, who never were under any illusions in the first place, pounced.

THE FUTURE

Thanks to the concerted and repeated efforts of advocates over the past three decades, Americans have grasped and internalized the truth: that gun policy is best made outside of crises, that the states are the best place for experimentation, and that the Left's preferred prescriptions tend, in this area at least, to be irrational or ignorant or both.

If it makes them feel better, progressives can pretend that the problem with the United States is the National Rifle Association or the gun manufacturers or those recalcitrant Americans who live in rural areas and will not bend to Hollywood's will. But the truth is rather more complex than that. Really, the NRA's only power is communicative. It tells voters whether or not candidates for office agree with them, and voters do the rest. Likewise, the role of gun manufacturers is to satisfy the people's demand for firearms. If people do not wish to own guns, their makers will go out of business. There is nothing in the American constitutional order that gives the firearms industry a vote. The NRA wins because it is popular.

How popular? Democrat Terry McAuliffe won the governor's race in Virginia last year by a few points: 48 percent to 45.5 percent. The NRA, meanwhile, polled at 51 percent favorability. Elsewhere the numbers are much higher, with the NRA outpolling the president in almost every state. Invoking the NRA might be a cheap way of getting people in

Manhattan and San Francisco to turn up their noses, but in most of the country the organization is viewed positively. News flash: People like their civil rights.

The Right should be extremely pleased with its progress in this area, not least because the gun issue is a powerful totem—an example that can be used to illustrate the integrity of a philosophy. Both conservatives and libertarians like to talk of fidelity to the Constitution, of a powerful and self-reliant citizenry, of local control, of the people knowing better what they need than does the state, of harsh reality trumping emotion and ideology, and of the vital importance of reformers electing to start from where they are and not where they would like to be. There are few better ways of illustrating a commitment to these ideals than to back the rights of the people on questions relating to deadly force.

Nevertheless, celebrants ought to be careful not to fall prey to complacency. The past two decades have yielded one of the few substantial policy reversals in American history, yes. But the nature of the American government is such that one knee-jerk reaction from an overzealous crop of Washington elites could wipe out decades' worth of gains at the stroke of a pen. It is no good slowly liberalizing gun laws at the state level if the feds can overrule your gains on a whim. The expired "assault weapons" ban of 1994 has been posthumously deemed a failure in major studies conducted by both the University of Pennsylvania and the Department of Justice. And yet it is favored still in blue states across the country, at the federal level by the likes of President Obama and Dianne Feinstein, and by a good number of Americans who have fallen prey to the propaganda. Concealed carry has

failed to yield any of the dangerous results that naysayers predicted it would. And yet we still hear know-nothings such as
Illinois governor Pat Quinn risibly claiming that if we "allow
private citizens to carry loaded, concealed handguns in public
places," and "you bump into somebody accidentally, well they
can pull out a loaded, concealed handgun to assuage their
anger." Nobody in the history of the United States has been
killed with a .50-caliber rifle, and yet they are still banned in
many states and are high on the gun controllers' hit list. Real
threats remain.

Advocates should set themselves five main goals for the
future. First, and always most important, is to hold the line
on recent victories. Public opinion is certainly on the Right's
side in this area, but tragedies invariably lead to short-lived
fluctuations, and all it would take for years of painstaking
work to be undone is a bad law passed hastily in anger. It
should be recognized that the majority of the victories that we
have enjoyed over the past few decades have been the product
of the states changing their laws and not of judges upholding
the federal Constitution. Those states could always change
the laws back. We must ensure that they do not.

Second, conservatives should attempt to build on the remarkable jurisprudential successes of the last decade. It is a
great blessing that the Supreme Court has recognized that
the Second Amendment to the Constitution protects an individual right, but there is still a great deal of work to be
done to ensure that that right is practically and meaningfully
protected. The 2008 *Heller* decision affirmed that private
gun ownership was protected by the Constitution, and the
2010 *McDonald* decision applied that principle to the states.

Nevertheless, the scope of the right, the weapons to which it pertains, and the manner in which lower courts must examine the underlying questions have never been established. Until the Supreme Court fleshes out its order, the right to keep and bear arms will be applied differently depending on where a citizen lives. Some of those who have found themselves stuck in states with hostile governments (California, Hawaii, Illinois) have managed to convince the courts that they are entitled to their rights, but others have been afforded no relief (New York, New Jersey, Connecticut). There is no doubt whatsoever that these issues will be taken up by the justices in the next few years. Conservatives must be ready.

Third, we must continue to educate the public against the misinformation on which our opponents have come to rely. The claim that America is in the midst of a gun-violence "epidemic" needs to be regularly debunked—and hard. Two reports, both released in May 2013, revealed a striking drop in gun crime over the past twenty years. The first, from the Department of Justice, confirmed that firearm-related homicides declined 39 percent between 1993 and 2011; that non-fatal firearm crimes declined 69 percent over the same time period; and that school shootings, too, were down 33 percent since 1993. The gains, the study showed, had been in every region of the country, and held true for all races and both sexes. The second, a Pew analysis of the same data, characterized gun-violence rates as being "strikingly lower" than they were in 1993, and recorded that "national rates of gun homicide, non-fatal gun crime and all non-fatal violent crimes have fallen since the mid-1990s."

Alas, as Pew noted:

Despite national attention to the issue of firearm violence, most Americans are unaware that gun crime is lower today than it was two decades ago. According to a new Pew Research Center survey, today 56% of Americans believe gun crime is higher than 20 years ago and only 12% think it is lower.

This is to say that Americans are unaware that, during the very period that gun laws have been dramatically liberalized across the whole country, gun crime has dropped substantially. For those who made asinine claims that reform would lead to Americans shooting one another in supermarket aisles, this has been deeply embarrassing. "Whenever a state legislature first considers a concealed-carry bill," Dave Kopel of the Independence Institute observed in 1996,

opponents typically warn of horrible consequences. But within a year of passage, the issue usually drops off the news media's radar screen, while gun-control advocates in the legislature conclude that the law wasn't so bad after all.

Almost twenty years later, these words are as true as ever. But there is no great virtue in the harbingers of doom being proved wrong if nobody is there to see it. Conservatives must ensure that Americans know that the predictions of the naysayers did not come to pass, and that gun-related crime has been almost cut in half while the laws have been liberalized.

Likewise, we must ensure that our critics do not get away with their slippery and selective use of crime statistics. Progressives like to tell the public that 30 thousand people are "killed with guns every year." Overall, this is true. But those wielding the number routinely fail to acknowledge that they are counting suicides *and* homicides in the same breath, thereby leaving an impression that is not quite right. A startling *two-thirds* of all fatal gunshot wounds are self-inflicted—a horrifically high number, of course, but one that changes the debate considerably. It is simply dishonest to conflate citizens making an awful personal choice with citizens being murdered, and it is patently absurd, too, to pretend that the problems have the same solution. Japan, which has probably the strictest gun-control laws in the world, has double the suicide rate as does the United States.

Conservatives should also make a point of insisting that emotional and meaningless terms such as "assault weapon" are called out whenever they are deployed. As anybody even vaguely familiar with firearms knows, there is no such thing as an "assault weapon." It is nothing more than an invented political term—a clever means by which cynical politicians might arbitrarily place any firearm that they wish to ban into a category that sounds troubling to the uninformed. "Assault weapon" does *not* mean "automatic weapon"—these are heavily regulated under federal law and are so rarely used in crimes as to represent a red herring—and it does *not* mean "more lethal." It means *nothing at all*, beyond "scary-looking gun that I don't like for reasons I can't quite explain."

Not only is the focus on "assault weapons" misleading, it is also a spectacular waste of everyone's time. When someone is killed with a gun in America, it is almost *certain* that a garden-variety handgun was used. Rifles of all sorts—not just so-called assault rifles—are used in around 3 percent of all killings. To put this into context, shotguns, which almost nobody is attempting to ban, are used in around 3.5 percent. Even if we use a maximalist definition of both "rifle" and "shotgun," it is the case that fewer people are shot annually in America with guns that are not handguns than are killed by *hands and fists*. As for those "assault" variants? They are utilized in so few murders each year that the federal government doesn't even bother to keep statistics.

Fourth, we should work to establish stronger reciprocal links between the states. Each of the fifty states is expected to respect my Connecticut driver's license. Why not my Connecticut concealed-carry permit? There are, it seems, three ways of achieving guaranteed reciprocity: It can be done on a bilateral "compact" basis between willing states, which is always preferable. It can be achieved via federal legislation that preempts those states and forces them to recognize one another's documents. Or it can be challenged in court under the Full Faith and Credit Clause of the Constitution. Personally, the latter two options make me uncomfortable: If we are to advocate for the power of the states, we must recognize that those states will be able to make decisions that we dislike. A better course, I think, is to work on reciprocity at the state level.

Finally, conservatives should continue to normalize guns and gun ownership. Outside of its obsession with "universal background checks," the gun-control brigade's latest trick is to lobby businesses and local governments to make gun bearers unwelcome in their stores and to put pressure on social media outlets to remove photographs of firearms from their users' pages. The intention here is obvious: to take firearms out of the cultural mainstream and to win in the private sector what they cannot achieve through government. We have already lost a lot of ground. As George Mason University's Walter E. Williams has noted, before the 1968 Gun Control Act was passed, "private transfers of guns to juveniles were unrestricted. Often a youngster's 12th or 14th birthday present was a shiny new .22-caliber rifle, given to him by his father." In the 1960s, school gun clubs were so common that, even in New York City, it was typical to see children walking to school with rifles slung over their backs. Nowadays students are suspended from school for making pistol shapes with their fingers or for simply saying "Bang!" in the schoolyard. Progressives widely mock "abstinence-only" sex education on the eminently reasonable grounds that sex is a fact of life and that children should therefore be taught about it. Why should abstinence-only *gun* education be immune from their derision?

A FINAL NOTE

On guns, as on so much else, the Left tends to discuss public policy in the abstract, insinuating at each point that the United States is little more than a sandbox game such as SimCity, with variables that can be tweaked and outcomes that can be painlessly altered by an omnipotent force possessed of good intentions and an infinite number of lives. It is no such thing. It is a living, breathing nation full of flawed people and imperfect institutions. In consequence, the material question before us is not "*Should* we live in a society with 350 million

guns and an entrenched constitutional right to gun ownership?" but "*Given* that we live in a country with 350 million
guns and a constitutional right to gun ownership, what *can* we
do to limit the violence?"

Here is the crux of the issue: There are simply far too
many firearms here for minor laws to make a difference,
while major laws are prohibited theoretically by the Constitution and practically by the culture. If there was ever a time in
which the United States could follow the example of a country such as Australia or Britain and collect up a significant
portion of the nation's guns, it has long passed. To institute
anything approaching a ban would be to invite a civil war and
the breaking apart of the American experiment. To do anything less is merely to irritate the law-abiding and to hand the
advantage to the criminal element. America is full of guns. It
is always going to be full of guns. Now that it is possible to
3D-print a gun, there is no way of preventing private ownership even if we wished to. On firearms, the ship has sailed.

Conservatives, meanwhile, might stop pretending that
there is no problem about which to be concerned. The blogger Andrew Sullivan told CNN's Anderson Cooper in 2013
that he was happy to acknowledge that the gun question
was intractable if advocates of the right to bear arms would
concede that this is not wholly positive. He was right. The
United States has more gun deaths than every other country
in the civilized world. This, obviously, is related to its citizenry's having almost half of the world's guns in their possession. Defenders of the Second Amendment gain nothing by
denying this.

On the contrary. Whatever the provocations in the media

or the demands of our mawkish political climate, conservatives must continue to ensure that they exhibit the same intellectual and moral honesty as did Professor Kleck. On the one hand, this requires us to steadfastly refuse to give in to fantasies and misconceptions that cost lives and strip people of their basic liberties. On the other, it means being precise with our language. Almost all legal gun owners are peaceful people, and the temptation to push against the hysterics is an understandable one. After all, if you are never going to hurt anybody, the suggestion that you are one wrong Starbucks order away from going postal will be inordinately frustrating to you. We should, however, avoid weakening our position by pretending that guns aren't deadly weapons that are designed deliberately and exclusively to kill and to maim. They are. Indeed, even if they are not fired, the *preventive* value of firearms is a function of their lethality. As George Orwell went to great pains to insist, a firearm in the hands of a good man does not cease to be a firearm; it just becomes a firearm used in a manner of which we approve.

The key question before us is not whether guns are dangerous—they really, really are—but *who gets them* in a free society. It makes little philosophical sense for the politicians whom the citizens of this free country have hired to represent them to be permitted to turn around and disarm their employers—especially when one remembers that the people's maintaining their right to bear arms was one of the preconditions of the social contract. The question of gun ownership is one of the most important and fundamental political questions of all, relating as it does to the allocation of the means of violence, the direction in which power is to flow, and the maintenance of the rule of law. Here, as elsewhere, conservatives should answer the question of who is to be privileged in the only way that is consistent with a free society: We, the People.

Which is ultimately to say that conservatives should recognize that this is not merely a question of economics. Along with the beautiful First Amendment, the Second Amendment is the most important philosophical statement in the whole of the United States Constitution. It must be jealously protected.

7

DRUGS: A STUDY IN FAILURE

IF you were to ask a politically ignorant visitor to the United States to examine the rhetoric of the country's main political movements, and to infer from this which of them was the most vehement advocate of the War on Drugs, the results would probably surprise you.

Think about what happens in America when reports of a mass shooting start dribbling in. In such cases, the self-identified conservatives reflexively privilege individual liberty over vague appeals to public safety. They laugh off the suggestion that inanimate objects—and not people—are responsible for bad deeds. They take offense at the implication that free citizens cannot be trusted to be responsible with potentially dangerous tools. They question whether the federal government even has the right to get involved, and note that such matters are supposed to be resolved locally. They seek to remind voters that conservative reforms have coincided with a staggering reduction in crime. They reject emotion and mawkishness, and refuse to subordinate good public policy to the catharsis of the aggrieved. And, most loudly of all perhaps, they balk at the conceit that authoritarian action can be an effective means of changing the behavior of a recalcitrant population. "If you liked Prohibition," one popular meme goes, "you'll love gun control."

Now think how conservatives tend to react to the issue of drugs in society. In this area, with a few virtuous exceptions, voters and public figures on the Right forget their political instincts and instead contrive arguments to fit their preferred outcomes. Here, conservatives allow the federal government to regulate drugs and to enforce punishments with a heavy hand. They ignore comprehensive data that shows the War on Drugs is failing. They strike a paternalistic tone that is out of keeping with their general message. They seem happy to abandon individual liberty in favor of wide-reaching and brutally enforced laws. And, disastrously, they are tone-deaf on the ways in which the issue involves the questions of poverty and of race.

In 2008, the GOP's national platform contained a commitment that, if elected to office, Republicans "will continue the fight against producers, traffickers, and distributors of illegal substances through the collaboration of state, federal, and local law enforcement." On firearms, meanwhile, the party struck a defiant note—promising to fight any and all intrusions on liberty and saying nothing of any substance as to how it might help to fight the problems of abuse and crime.

This is intellectually inconsistent and politically dishonest. By its own account, the Right is motivated by a respect for local control and a passion for individual freedom. When *drugs* are the issue, however, it readily abandons both, cheering on the very government that it routinely dismisses as overbearing and turning a blind eye to the suffering that the War on Drugs has caused.

On first examination at least, "drug *choice*" would seem to be a much better emblem for conservatives to recommend, would it not? Not only might this make better law, but the issue, as does gun control, could serve as a useful totem for conservatism—a practical example with which to communicate a philosophy and to lay out strong positions on liberty, federalism, governmental restraint, personal responsibility, historical precedent, the difference between the morality of the state and of the individual, and the age-old tradition of minding your own damn business. Certainly, drugs can ruin lives. That much is undeniable. But since when has this been a convincing argument for the Don't Tread on Me crowd?

National Review's founder, William F. Buckley Jr., coined a useful aphorism. What "is legal," Buckley wrote, "is not necessarily reputable." Here he was pushing back at the fundamentally statist conceit that the government must be the arbiter of all public morality—a notion best summed up by the fatuous claim that "if you make something legal, everyone will start doing it." Buckley's phrase is a profitable one, not least because it highlights the space that exists between agitating for liberty and endorsing the consequences. The merits of doing so to one side, it should be perfectly clear to those on the Right that to end the failed War on Drugs would no more require opponents of drug use to relinquish their stead-fast opposition than to refuse to punish the Ku Klux Klan for exercising its right to free speech requires us to cease oppos-ing white supremacy. As government grows and civil society recedes, establishing in the public imagination that to allow something is not to endorse it becomes increasingly crucial. There is an opportunity here.

The first question is philosophical. To anyone who has been paying attention, it is evident that defense of the War on Drugs is "conservative" only in the worst sense of that word. People are starting to notice. Even Pat Robertson, the South-ern Baptist media guru and bogeyman of the hard-line Chris-tian Right, has woken up (although he blames the wrong people). "Every time the liberals pass a bill—I don't care what it involves—they stick criminal sanctions on it," Robertson argued in a 2012 interview with the *New York Times*. In conse-quence, he complained, Americans "make up 5 percent of the world's population, but we make up 25 percent of jailed pris-oners." His solution? "I really believe we should treat mari-juana the way we treat . . . alcohol."

Once upon a time, we did. It was the Right's archenemy, that progressive hero and enemy of classical liberalism, Presi-dent Woodrow Wilson, who signed the federal Harrison Narcotics Tax Act in 1914, and thereby put an end to the widespread and free availability of drugs. Until the first two decades of the twentieth century, marijuana, opium, cocaine, and heroin had all been legal and unregulated—not because the government deigned to "allow" the citizenry to enjoy them, but because nobody had ever suggested that the federal government had any legitimate role in their regulation in the first place. It seems astonishing today that, as late as 1890, Americans could buy cocaine and a syringe with which to inject it from the Sears mail-order catalog. At the time, however, that was just how America worked. Progressives, who sought to shred the Constitution's protections and to replace them with a more efficient and centralized state, put an end to that, as they would also do later to the availability of alcohol and prostitution.

The *American Conservative*'s Anthony Gregory has observed that it is peculiar that the War on Drugs is acceptable to anyone who professes to be concerned with limited government and respect for local preferences, for it "embodies secular leviathan like few other government efforts." It should be no surprise that President Obama has proved so disappointing to reformers on this issue. Despite his carefully cultivated image, he is a reflexive authoritarian, for whom the answer to every problem is always government intervention. Of *course* he is a drug warrior.

But why are conservatives? In 2010, Republicans issued a "Pledge to America," in which they promised to "honor the Constitution as constructed by its framers and honor the original intent of those precepts that have been consistently ignored—particularly the Tenth Amendment." What better way of doing this than to call for the federal government to scale back its drug war and leave the question of regulation to the states? Nowhere in either the "Constitution as constructed by its framers," nor in the *Federalist Papers* that were written to explain and to defend the document-as-constructed, is there any hint whatsoever that the federal government ought to be worrying itself over which substances free citizens may put into their bodies. Neither, as the Mises Institute's Laurence M. Vance has noted, is there any suggestion that the federal government was intended to boast a National Drug Control Strategy, National Survey on Drug Use and Health, Domestic Cannabis Eradication/Suppression Program, Substance Abuse and Mental Health Services Administration, Office of National Drug Control Policy, or Drug Enforcement Administration or to put onto the swelling books a Controlled Substances Act, Comprehensive Drug Abuse Prevention and Control Act, or Combat Methamphetamine Epidemic Act—all of which, the Cato Institute's Jeffrey A. Miron estimates, cost around $41 billion per annum.

Now, this is not to say that conservatives should be "pro-drug." Indeed, the beauty of opposing *federal* involvement is that it affords us a free hand elsewhere. Conservatives can quite happily agitate for federal withdrawal *and* continue to argue against the wisdom of using drugs *and* leave the legal questions to the states and localities. The whole *point* of America's system of government is that the decisions that matter should be made as close as possible to the people those decisions affect. The Right makes much of federalism and of the overreaching and negative influence of the national government. Imagine how revolutionary the Republican Party would seem if it were to start campaigning for full local choice on this matter. Imagine which constituencies it might convince to give the movement a second look. Imagine, too, how powerful it would be to see conservatives demonstrating that what they personally want and what they think the government should do are not one and the same. If we are to have a War on Drugs, shouldn't it be run by the governments that actually have the power to wage it: those of the states? And if we are to have a system in place to react to what is already a real problem, shouldn't it be one driven by civil society? America benefits immensely from the network of families, churches, charities, and volunteers that attempt to mitigate the consequences of addiction and to prevent those who might struggle with it from ever becoming too far entangled. Let's use them.

Thus far, alas, conservatives have been part of the problem, sometimes leading and other times following attempts to inject the state into the question. The War on Drugs has been one of the great bipartisan efforts of the last century. Democrats presided over the Marijuana Tax Act of 1937, and Lyndon Johnson's hideous Great Society power grab brought more rules into the fold. Republican Richard Nixon signed the 1970 Controlled Substances Act, which formalized the prohibition of almost every conceivable drug, and Ronald Reagan signed a bill that greatly expanded the penalties for its violation. For his part, Bill Clinton upped the number of marijuana arrests, and Barack Obama, apparently unimpressed by the way in which George W. Bush had deprioritized drug enforcement spending, included a sizeable increase in the 2009 "stimulus." Next time somebody saccharinely praises politicians for "working together," remember that.

IT is worth acknowledging that the impulse to regulate and to prohibit certain substances did not spring up for no good reason. As we should all know by now, drugs are in fact rather bad for you. Marijuana tends to make people inordinately stupid and irritating, and it can seriously impair driving, chronically lower productivity, and—if the strain is strong enough—cause permanent damage to the brain. While drug legalizers are right to point out that nobody in the history of recorded medicine has ever died from a marijuana *overdose*, this doesn't tell the full story. Simply because a man is not killed by it does not mean that a drug, used habitually, has no serious consequences. Several studies have shown that heavy use of weed is linked with relationship problems, diminished academic and professional success, and a higher likelihood of dropping out of school. The same goes for harder drugs, with which the consequences tend to be amplified, and which are usually lethal if taken in a large enough dose.

There is, I think, a reasonable case to be made that anybody who cares either about individualism or about a flourishing civil society would wish to keep their fellow citizens away from substances that subvert their capacity to make rational decisions. As the British doctor-turned-writer Anthony Daniels has proposed, sometimes it is inappropriate to argue on the grounds of liberty for the legalization of substances that serve primarily to take the exercise of that liberty away. "The consumption of drugs," Daniels writes,

> has the effect of reducing men's freedom by circumscribing the range of their interests. It impairs their ability to pursue more important human aims, such as raising a family and fulfilling civic obligations. Very often it impairs their ability to pursue gainful employment and promotes parasitism. Moreover, far from being expanders of consciousness, most drugs severely limit it. One of the most striking characteristics of drug takers is their intense and

tedious self-absorption; and their journeys into inner space
are generally forays into inner vacuums. Drug taking is
a lazy man's way of pursuing happiness and wisdom, and
the shortcut turns out to be the deadest of dead ends. We
lose remarkably little by not being permitted to take drugs.

I cannot say that I disagree with Daniels's normative assessment much, which is one of the reasons that I do not take drugs. Here the impulse to "do something" is a noble and comprehensible one, born of a legitimate humanitarian instinct and worthy of our consideration. And yet there is a crucial difference between saying "Society would be better off if drugs vanished overnight" and saying "Society is better off when the government tries to make drugs vanish." When one compares the potential consequences of drugs being more widely and legally available with the very real consequences yielded by the drug war, the calculation must change considerably. We are not operating from a position of strength, in which drugs are all happily illegal and the crazy libertarians are asking apropos of nothing whether this makes philosophical sense; we are living in a country in which millions of people already use drugs *and* in which we suffer the consequences of trying to stop them. Contrary to Daniels's calculation, we lose a *lot* "by not being permitted to take drugs."

Similarly worth consideration is the argument that big government has created a status quo within which reform will be extremely tricky. As I argued in an earlier chapter, a flaw with the libertarianism to which I largely subscribe is the tendency of its adherents to pretend that they are dealing with a blank slate. They are not. The truth is that, if one's employment and health care are to be turned into the financial problems of others, others will demand a say in how you live. Just as the British National Health Service used to harangue me about how much wine I was drinking—and felt justified in doing so on the grounds that I was potentially costing it money and resources—Americans have a point when they say that they don't have a problem with drugs *per se*, but neither do they want the consequences of drug use added to the vast welfare system. As with the other criticisms, I would contend that the problems being created by the outlawing of drugs far and away outstrip the potential problems with legalization. However, the "look at the status quo" contingent does have a point.

But not, I am afraid, enough of one. Legal drugs may be bad news, and the size of the state may complicate reform, but that reform is almost certainly preferable to the maintenance of our current regime. What are we to make, for example, of the disastrous effect that mandatory minimum sentencing has had on African Americans, who live disproportionately in poor and crime-ridden areas and who make up half of all state drug-crime-related prisoners? What are we to make of the impact that incarcerating so many people—often merely for possession of negligible amounts of narcotics—has on families, the breakup of which condemns countless children to growing up with only one of their parents or, worse, in foster care? What are we to make of putting nonviolent offenders in with the violent and the professionally criminal, where they might enjoy a master class in criminal techniques?

What are we to make of so many nonviolent citizens being stripped of their voting rights and of the right to bear arms on the basis of what can be a single youthful indiscretion? What are we to make of the fact that spending on prisons is second only to Medicaid as the fastest-growing area of state budgets? What are we to make of the violence that has been done to privacy rights and to the Fourth Amendment? What are we to make of the undermining of the important principles of federalism and of enumerated powers? Are we to assume that these things are just minor downsides to a worthwhile program? Or are we perhaps to recognize that there is so much on the other side of the ledger already that we are getting almost nothing for our buck?

"Over all," writes the *New Yorker*'s Adam Gopnik, "there are now more people under 'correctional supervision' in America—more than 6 million—than were in the Gulag Archipelago under Stalin at its height." Sadly, this is not hyperbole or propaganda. The U.S. has a quite astonishing prison population: around 760 prisoners per 100,000 citizens. That's higher than almost every other developed country. Britain, by way of a reasonable comparison, has 153.

When Jimmy Carter left office in 1980, the prison population was 150 per 100,000, a number that he considered sufficiently alarming to prompt him to suggest that marijuana should be decriminalized. Since that time, the Congressional Research Service reports, the federal prison population has increased almost 790 percent. Sentencing has been extended dramatically, with mandatory minimum sentences being extended, enforcement hardened, and parole eliminated in large part. In 2010, half of all federal prisoners were in for drug offenses, and a staggering 93.6 percent of all inmates were serving time for nonviolent crimes. One-third of all federal prisoners are first-time nonviolent offenders. Meanwhile, drug use has stayed somewhat level, and in recent years actually increased. This is failure on a massive scale.

Conservatives tend to worry about the effect that government intrusion can have on the marketplace, and to note with frustration that the most likely response to a failed government initiative is the expansion of that government initiative. Why not here? Illegal drugs are, without doubt, significantly more expensive simply because they are illegal. The small scale of production and the high risks involved inevitably raise the price. A paper produced by Jeffrey Miron for the University of Chicago suggested that heroin is 70 times as expensive on the street as it would be if produced legally. Cocaine, he argues, would cost 20 times less; marijuana 15 times less. Intervention makes a difference.

Some reading these statistics will presumably conclude that this is a good thing. After all, if you want to stop people from taking drugs, that they are out of reach for most people is an indication of success, right? Well, no, not really. As with firearms, making something illegal does not eliminate demand for it, and in the case of expensive drugs, high prices often have the effect of pushing users into crime. Addicts desperate for a fix are forced to resort to theft, involvement in gangs, prostitution, and drug dealing to get what they crave. Prohibition, meanwhile, creates a ready-made black market into which the down and out are sucked. "Drugs," Columbia University's John McWhorter suggests, "make thugs":

> The gangs' main activity is selling drugs, which can be sold
> at a markup because they are illegal. If the drugs were not

illegal and available in clinics in moderate doses while re-
habilitation was widely available, these men couldn't sell
the drugs on the street. As such, they would have no reason
to fight over turf with guns, and therefore would neither
be killing each other nor poised to be killed by white cops.

Criminalization thus leads to criminality, and the imprisonment of criminals leads to more criminality, creating a vicious cycle, the response to which has usually been increased funding for law enforcement, ever more aggressive attempts to interfere, and a vast colony of American prisoners. Naturally, that colony does not imprison itself. In order to build it, many of America's local police forces have begun to resemble armored divisions. As American involvement in the Middle East has wound down, the presence of surplus military equipment—including armored vehicles, tanks, grenades, body armor, and fully automatic weapons—has become standard in many cities here at home as police chiefs desperate to keep up with the drug dealers' latest gadgetry have rapaciously acquired whatever they could get their hands on. In the process, the Fourth Amendment has taken a savage beating. As Radley Balko documents in horrifying detail in his recent book, *Rise of the Warrior Cop*, the number of warrantless searches, nighttime raids, SWAT team attacks, and unnecessary killings has increased dramatically since 1970.

The ACLU reports that, each year, American SWAT teams conduct more than 45,000 raids—about 124 per day (or, rather, per night). Only 7 percent of these raids are made in response to riots, active shooters, or hostage situations—the three eventualities for which such teams are assembled. A remarkable four in five, however, are performed so that authorities can "search homes, usually for drugs." Conservatives and libertarians alike should be worried about this. There is no point in our enjoying strict rules prohibiting the military from roaming America's streets if our police forces are going to reconstruct themselves as the ersatz 101st Airborne.

Whatever their view on drugs *per se*, the severe practical consequences of the War on Drugs should prompt conservatives to reexamine their assumptions. Whether they know it or not, they are perfectly placed to do so. This is the movement that was brave enough to stand up against the superficial do-gooder mantra of gun control and to argue successfully that it was hindering, not helping, attempts to fight crime. This is the movement that pointed out, to a chorus of disapprobation, that the War on Poverty was pouring money down the drain and that truth could not be subordinated to good intentions for long. This is the movement that pushed Bill Clinton to sign a welfare reform bill and, when that measure was shown to be a roaring success, proved wrong the most dramatic of its opponents' predictions. This is the movement that observed that tax rates were important because, while total revenues seem to remain pretty much static regardless of the brackets, they can have a real effect on economic growth.

If conservatives have a key strength, it is the ability to look at an issue with a dispassionate eye and to appraise the performance of government as they would anything else. They are the people who speak as a first language federalism, individual liberty, personal responsibility, and the limitation of state power. Theirs is the movement accustomed to taking on sacred cows and to reforming government when it is no longer working. Can we honestly say that the involvement of government in the drug war is making things better?

The good news is that, slow as it might be, change is afoot. The 1980s and 1990s yielded a political environment in which, for understandable reasons, politicians were skittish about being seen as soft on the crime with which Americans had become so rightly fed up. From the 1970s onwards, the federal government instituted harsh mandatory minimum sentencing for drug possession and use, and most states followed suit. But the crash of 2008 provoked many of those states into reexamining their budgets, and the relatively low crime rate allowed those lawmakers to propose reform without deathly fear of losing their seats.

Retrenchment always provides an opportunity for re-evaluation. When mocking conservatives, Joe Biden is fond of saying "Show me your budget and I will know your values." One suspects that the vice president knows not how true these words are. When times are good there is an unfortunate human tendency for nations to simply move forward inexorably. When the money runs out and things get tough, choices must be made and priorities established. Are conservatives prepared to look at the cost and the consequences—both to liberty and to the taxpayer—and say that the War on Drugs is worth it?

IF the Right is searching for an example of how they might wage this battle, it might forgo the usual suspects and look instead to Pauline Sabin, a reforming member of the Republican National Committee during the early twentieth century.

Sabin was initially wooed by the "word-pictures of the agita-tors" and was supportive of Prohibition in consequence, but she changed her mind as the bodies piled up. "I thought a world without liquor would be a beautiful world," Sabin re-ported. "I felt I should approve of it because it would help my two sons."

By 1929, she no longer did. "Children are growing up with a total lack of respect for the Constitution and for the law," Sabin repined. "The young see the law broken at home and upon the street. Can we expect them to be lawful?" After President Hoover signed the Jones-Stalker Act in May of that year, drastically increasing the punishment for the consump-tion of alcohol and doubling down on what was a clear failure, Sabin quit the RNC in frustration and formed the Women's Organization for National Prohibition Reform. The Repub-lican Party, meanwhile, vacillated between indifference and vehemence, the result of which was to leave Franklin Delano Roosevelt, the man who presided over the biggest and most centralizing expansion of government in American history, to pick up the mantle of reform and of freedom and to stand smiling in front of the cameras, touting repeal as his baby.

It should not make the same mistake this time around.

8

THE MYTH OF
"SOCIAL ISSUES"

———◆———

Ask an armchair pundit what is holding back
the Republican Party and he will almost certainly smile a lupine smile and mention "social
conservatism." Insofar as there is one, the argument runs something like this: Young people
would be willing to get on board with the GOP
if only the GOP would drop its old-fashioned
views on matters of "morality." As it is, new
voters are put off at the first hurdle, thereby declining to consider Republicans' views on issues
relating to taxation, the size and influence of
the government, the balance of power between
Washington, D.C., and the states, the severity
of business and environmental regulation, the
integrity and sustainability of the social safety
net, the role of the United States in the world,

and the cost of health care—questions on which they are, or could be, sympathetic to the conservative point of view.

There is some truth in this statement, but it needs an awful lot of unpacking. For a start, we might ask what we mean by the term "social issues." Politically advantageous as it can be to lump together under one banner the questions of abortion, gay marriage, and the legalization of drugs, the topics are in fact philosophically discrete. The conservative case against abortion is a remarkably simple one, predicated upon a steadfast opposition to the taking of human life. Conservative opposition to both gay marriage and the legal availability of drugs, by contrast, is driven by a desire to ensure the integrity and health of society. This is a distinction that is typically ignored.

The issues are psephologically separate, too. While public opinion is increasingly behind progressives on the questions of gay marriage and drugs, support for legal abortion is going in the other direction—not just among the population at large, but among young voters, also. When we say that "young people are socially liberal," we really mean that they are strongly in favor of gay marriage and legal weed and . . . well, that's about it. Indeed, as a 2014 Reason-Rupe poll discovered, in the minds of the young, the word "liberal" *on its own* might primarily mean this, too. A *Time* magazine feature interpreting the survey, written by *Reason*'s Nick Gillespie, noted that "about 62% of Millennials call themselves *liberal*." "By that," he observed, "they mean they favor gay marriage and pot legalization, but those views hold little or no implication for their views on government spending. To Millennials, being socially liberal is being liberal, period."

If "socially liberal" means "supports gay marriage and pot," then we can say without a doubt that the social liberals are winning. In 2014, Pew Research found that 69 percent of Americans between the ages of 18 and 29 "[favored] allowing gays and lesbians to marry legally," among them a remarkable *61 percent* of self-described Republicans (77 percent of Democrats of the same age are pro). This number stands in stark contrast to Republicans between the ages of 30 and 49 (43 percent in favor), between 50 and 64 (30 percent in favor), and over 65 (22 percent in favor). On the question of same-sex marriage, Pew concluded, "young Republicans' views are more in line with Democrats." And, it seems, with the country at large. At last count, 54 percent of Americans considered themselves to be on board with the change.

Marijuana is pretty much the same story, with legalization enjoying exactly the same level of support as gay marriage: 54 percent. A (separate) Pew poll from 2014 revealed that 70 percent of Americans between the ages of 18 and 29 believe that the drug should "be legal," and that 81 percent of that age group believe it to be less "harmful to a person's health" than is alcohol. The split between young and older Republicans is not quite as pronounced here—a *New York Times*/CBS poll from February 2014 reported that 43 percent of Republicans under 45 were in favor of legalization while just 28 percent of those age 45 and over agreed. But the difference is still notable.

Abortion, however, remains a complicated outlier. According to Gallup, 48 percent of Americans describe themselves as being "pro-life," while 44 percent plump for "pro-choice." Somewhat revealingly, Americans seem to believe that this is the other way around—a fact that may help to explain why abortion is lumped in with other issues that are trending away from the Right. Asking the public to describe "how most Americans feel about abortion," Gallup discovered that "51% of U.S. adults say the public is mostly 'pro-choice,' while 35% say 'pro-life.' This general perception that the pro-choice viewpoint prevails contrasts with the nearly even division of Americans' actual views."

Unlike with drugs and gay marriage, on abortion young people do not diverge from the attitudes of other generations. A 35-year study, concluded by Gallup in 2010, discovered that the only Americans more opposed to abortion than 18- to 29-year-olds were those over 65—and even then the difference was tiny. This, the research concluded, represents a "sharp change from the late 1970s, when seniors were substantially more likely than younger age groups to want abortion to be illegal." Gallup's takeaway from the survey? "Americans aged 18 to 29 [are] trending more anti-abortion."

If anything, this is likely to lead to a *strengthening* of the laws governing abortion, rather than a liberalization. One of the most underreported phenomena in American politics is just how out of touch with public opinion the country's abortion regulations are. "A solid majority of Americans (61%)," Gallup notes,

> *believe abortion should generally be legal in the first three months of pregnancy, while 31% disagree. However support drops off sharply, to 27%, for second-trimester abortions, and further still, to 14%, for third-trimester abortions. Gallup has found this pattern each time it has*

asked this question since 1996, indicating that Americans attach much greater value to the fetus as it approaches viability, starting in the second trimester.

Suffice it to say that American abortion law looks nothing like this. Most states permit terminations until *twenty weeks* and beyond, and proposals to limit the practice even to the first five months are met with extraordinary resistance from the Left—despite their popularity with the public at large. As the *New York Times*'s David Leonhardt has argued, "on abortion rights, *both parties* have a claim on public opinion" (emphasis mine):

> *If you were going to craft a law based strictly on public opinion, it would permit abortion in the first trimester (first 12 weeks) of pregnancy and in cases involving rape, incest or threats to the mother's health. The law, however, would substantially restrict abortion after the first trimester in many other cases.*

So, why doesn't it? Why is there no movement to establish in the Constitution or elsewhere a rule that splits the difference?

The answer, I'd venture, is that the issue is not one that lends itself to either compromise or accommodation. For all the complicated epithets and self-serving psychoanalysis that is thrown at the pro-life movement and its political enablers, its position is a devastatingly simple one: that an unborn life counts as a life and thus deserves the same protections that would be accorded to a human being outside of the womb.

The exact details of this contention may change slightly, as might the manner in which it is applied to the law, to medicine, and to the culture at large. Political preferences vary, too. But the fundamental idea does not. For conservatives, abortion has nothing to do with the question of "women's rights," of family planning, or of how we might best organize our society, but is instead inextricable from the most basic and timeless of ethical questions: *When, and what, is it acceptable to kill?*

This topic invites an extraordinary amount of fluff and hand waving, but really there is only one important question to be resolved: Are pro-lifers correct in their claim that an unborn child is "a life," and if so, is that life worth more than the mother's preferences? To these questions must be subjugated all ancillary inquiries about the merits and demerits of adoption, the health of the economy, the nature of the state, the impact of population growth on the climate, the crime rate, the virtues of having children who are born into poverty or into families that do not want or love them, the career prospects of women, the problem of income inequality, the integrity of the social safety net, and any number of the remaining utilitarian concerns that are typically deployed to distract from the issue. Once one has acknowledged that pro-lifers believe that they are discussing the murder of human beings, an appeal to consequence makes sense only if one would be willing to suggest murder as a policy remedy in the case of children and adults, too. It is possible, of course, that murdering the indigent and the disabled would reduce the federal deficit and lower the rising cost of housing. It is feasible, too, that a well-executed program to cull motorists would ease traffic congestion. But we do not discuss these things in earnest because we agree almost universally that murdering people is wrong. (Indeed, many among us—myself included—contend that it is so wrong that we should not even be executing serial killers in the name of the public good.) Abortion is a "social issue" only if it is not murder. If it is, it is no more categorizable in that manner than is genocide.

A handful on the pro-choice side are happy to discuss the issue as it should be discussed, arguing either that there is no life involved until a pregnancy has reached a particular point, or conceding happily that life begins at conception but nonetheless asking "So what?" Most of those who advocate for the practice, however, are not prepared to take on either case. There is a simple reason that advocates rely upon euphemisms such as "women's equality," "women's rights," "reproductive rights," "reproductive justice," "pro-choice," and so forth; that they pretend they are discussing "health" and not death; and that they accuse their opponents of "hating" women, of wishing to return them to "second-class" status, or of having a dastardly secret agenda that public opposition to abortion serves only to mask. That simple reason? The truth hurts.

Still, cowardly as it is, argument by euphemism is a remarkably effective tactic for the advocates of abortion on demand. Engaging honestly with the question, by contrast, does not tend to work out well. In 2013, a writer named Mary Elizabeth Williams penned an essay for the website Salon titled "So What If Abortion Ends Life?" and in doing so, unleashed something of a firestorm. Consider this passage from her piece:

Of all the diabolically clever moves the anti-choice lobby has ever pulled, surely one of the greatest has been its consistent co-opting of the word "life." Life! Who wants to argue with that? Who wants to be on the side of . . . not-life? That's why the language of those who support abortion has for so long been carefully couched in other terms. While opponents of abortion eagerly describe themselves as "pro-life," the rest of us have had to scramble around with not nearly as big-ticket words like "choice" and "reproductive freedom." The "life" conversation is often too thorny to even broach. Yet I know that throughout my own pregnancies, I never wavered for a moment in the belief that I was carrying a human life inside of me. I believe that's what a fetus is: a human life. And that doesn't make me one iota less solidly pro-choice.

This is a startling admission—one that must have driven the more intellectually honest of her fellow travelers to drink. Yes, Williams had the courage to concede, an unborn child is a life. *But I am happy to kill it anyway*—not, you will note, in order to save the life of the mother (a wholly reasonable position that pits two competing lives against one another) but, as she wrote later in the column, to protect "the roads that women who have choice then get to go down" and to preserve the expanded "possibilities for them and for their families." The answer to Williams's rhetorical question "Who wants be on the side of . . . not-life?" is "Williams." Unlike her comrades, she just has the courage to admit it.

You will observe, too, that Williams does not consider the pro-life movement to be "diabolical" for having chosen a name for itself that is misleading or imprecise; she deems it unsporting for having selected a "big-ticket" word that is entirely appropriate to its cause. That is to say, her criticism of her opponents' use of the word "life" is not akin to my problem with the Left's use of the word "liberal"—my objection being that progressives have appropriated a moniker that does not belong to them—but that their honesty in advertising has left her to "scramble around" looking for a way to avoid acknowledging the truth. Conceding that abortion ends a life is difficult for people like her "to talk about," she writes, "lest we wind up looking like death-panel-loving, kill-your-grandma-and-your-precious-baby storm troopers." Again, you will detect the obvious: Williams is not concerned that her position makes her the bad guy; she is concerned that it makes her "look like" it.

While one suspects that she did not set out to do so, Williams demonstrated perfectly both why abortion is different than most "social issues" and why conservatives cannot merely consent to its permanence as the price of electoral success. In politics, negotiaton is often a virtue. There are a few areas, however, in which one is unable to seek moderation. This is one of them.

In order to present her defense, Williams is forced not only to justify what no respecter of human life can ever be asked to accept—that the convenience of the powerful should be held to be more important than the very *lives* of the powerless—but also to deny wholesale that there is such a thing as objective reality, respect for which should serve as the cornerstone of one's politics. When Williams argues that the mother is "the boss" of her unborn child, and that "her life and what is right for her circumstances and her health should automatically trump the rights of the non-autonomous entity inside of her . . . always," she is simultaneously stating that it would be acceptable for that "boss" to kill her child right up to the point at which it was born *and* suggesting that the value of the child is merely what the mother *says* it is—a claim that cannot survive reasonable scrutiny. My life is more important than that of my dog, and my dog relies upon me for life. Does this mean that I can unilaterally decide whether my dog is a dog or not? Of course I cannot.

That way spells disaster—both for individuals and for society at large. As the writer Elizabeth Scalia noted at the time, Williams's position is "precisely the utilitarian argument made by every totalitarian ideology that ever slaughtered people by the millions, because they were the wrong sorts of people, or were useless eaters, or they could not contribute to the advancement of society, or their quality of life just seemed too dubious to those who did not know and love them."

Scalia's critique pushes us to remember what has happened throughout history when the value of life has been deemed to be variable. But it should also raise some questions closer to home. Astonishingly, in some American states, Williams's relativist position is actually *codified into law*. In 2013, when the serial kidnapper and rapist Ariel Castro was finally discovered by police and forced to confront his crimes, prosecutors in Ohio mulled seeking the death penalty for "aggravated murder." Castro, as anyone who followed the case will remember, did not actually kill any of his kidnappees. He *did*, however, kill at least one of their unborn children. Ohio's legal system regards unborn children as potential murderees.

Castro was eventually charged with two counts of "aggravated murder," and, had the prosecution sought it, under Ohio's law he could legally have been executed for having ended the lives of his captives' unborn children. And yet, in Ohio as everywhere else in the United States, abortion is legal. Think upon this for a moment. An American state has erected a legal regime in which someone who kills an unborn child with the mother's permission is a free man providing a medical service, but someone who kills an unborn child without the mother's permission is a "murderer" whose crime is regarded as being so heinous that he can be killed himself. As a matter of criminal law, Ohio has not just entrenched the right of a mother to kill her child, but given institutional succor to the idea that a life is only a life if the mother says it is a life.

This approach should be resisted at all costs. The insistence that one cannot subordinate external reality to one's political preferences is utterly crucial to the integrity of individual liberty and to the maintenance of the individual right to conscience. In his seminal essay "Politics and the English Language," George Orwell lamented that political language of all kinds "is designed to make lies sound truthful and murder respectable, and to give an appearance of solidity to pure wind." Admirably, Williams seems at one level to agree, suggesting that her comrades on the pro-choice side are drawing meaningless semantic distinctions in order to justify their behavior, and that blunt truths would be a preferable course:

I have friends who have referred to their abortions in terms of "scraping out a bunch of cells" and then a few years later were exultant over the pregnancies that they unhesitatingly described in terms of "the baby" and "this kid." I know women who have been relieved at their abortions and grieved over their miscarriages. Why can't we agree that how they felt about their pregnancies was vastly different, but that it's pretty silly to pretend that what was growing inside of them wasn't the same? Fetuses aren't selective like that. They don't qualify as human life only if they're intended to be born.

She drives the point home:

When we try to act like a pregnancy doesn't involve human life, we wind up drawing stupid semantic lines in the sand: first trimester abortion vs. second trimester vs. late term, dancing around the issue trying to decide if there's a single magic moment when a fetus becomes a person. Are you human only when you're born? Only when you're viable outside of the womb? Are you less of a human life when you look like a tadpole than when you can suck on your thumb?

She is right, which makes it all the more peculiar that she appears incapable of recognizing that this line of thought serves to bolster her opponents' case and not her own. After all, if we should avoid "drawing stupid semantic lines in the sand" and "trying to decide if there's a single magic moment when a fetus becomes a person," then why should we believe that it is wrong for a parent to kill their child ten minutes after it has been born? Certainly, a newborn baby is slightly less dependent on the mother than it was in utero. But it doesn't enjoy immediate autonomy. For a long while, babies rely upon their parents for almost everything. Can we off them if they aren't going to be wanted? No, we cannot. Not, that is, unless we are happy to, in Orwell's words, make "murder respectable" and to allow our critics to make the wind solid. That even pro-choicers like Williams are reluctant to describe abortion in non-obscurative terms is, one might guess, one reason why public opinion is trending toward conservatives' positions on the issue.

MOVING FORWARD

It should by now be painfully clear that Americans who oppose abortion cannot and will not adjust their position to suit the political zeitgeist, as they could on, say, marginal tax rates or the contents of the school curriculum. Nor, for that matter, can they take an "each to his or her own" approach. If one believes that killing is wrong and that abortion is killing, there is no alternative but for the state to step in and prevent it. As there is no "libertarian" or "moderate" case against the prohibition of murder, there is no magic means by which conservatives might throw up their hands and say, "Oh well." Forty years after *Roe v. Wade*, the debate still rages. It almost certainly always will.

Nevertheless, conservatives can do a much better job at explaining their case. Sincere as it is in its opposition, the pro-life movement has to take most of the blame for the perception that its opposure to abortion is inextricably linked either with specific religious beliefs or with social conservatism in general. By allowing the issue to be made synonymous with a broader piety, pro-lifers have criminally undermined their case with the wider electorate, making it appear that the only reason one might oppose abortion is that one believes in God and allowing themselves to be cast as dissenters on the margins rather than as representatives of a slim but firm majority. The movement has, in other words, chosen the wrong words for making the right case.

That case can be made. Pro-lifers are never going to win over those who believe that womanhood is a victim status, nor should they try. But they may well make inroads with the rest. I am an atheist who is in favor of gay marriage, who is opposed to the continuation of the War on Drugs, and who has no objections whatsoever to contraception outside of its being mandated. But it has never been difficult for me to take Ockham's razor to the issue of life—that is, to remove both social conservative and religious variables from the equation and to be left with a simple, coherent, and persuasive argument that a life is a life and that anybody who is interested in individual liberty is duty bound to protect the innocent. As a rule, Americans are unaware not only that the pro-life movement represents the majority but that it is growing, and they are uninformed as to how wildly out of step our laws are with public sentiment. If there is a single task to which the opponents of abortion on demand should commit themselves, it is to remedying this nescience.

Second, conservatives should allow more readily that they are living in a culture in which the practice of some form of abortion is widely accepted, and in which most people are happy for it to remain legal—during the first trimester at least. If progressives overestimate the extent to which their extremism is supported by the mainstream—and they absolutely do—conservatives can overstate the scale of the support for their restrictions. Even if the general public came to agree that abortion was morally wrong in all circumstances, it would likely balk at the prospect of outlawing it completely.

There would be some wisdom in this reluctance. Were *Roe* to be abruptly overturned tomorrow, thereby freeing the states to establish their own abortion policies, the essential problem would remain: that summarily banning a common activity is extraordinarily difficult—and, as history shows, often practically disastrous. Slavery, perhaps the greatest evil of them all, was abolished in America only by an unimaginably disruptive and bloody civil war, while the international trade that supported it was brought to an end courtesy of British gunboats and their commanders' willingness to use them. That so many people believe that abortion on demand is acceptable is a travesty. But it is also the truth. This has consequences.

Legal reform is necessary—conservatives should prioritize enacting rules that require that abortion clinics hew to standard medical practices and bring rules more closely into sympathy with the public's preferences—but this is a battle that will eventually be won not by drying up the supply but by eliminating the demand. Evils are more effectively sent to the margins by private disgust than by public punishment. Want a constructive plan? Continue to win hearts and minds.

In this aim, modern medicine is the friend, not the enemy, of pro-lifers. We are now capable of watching unborn children hiccup, yawn, and laugh in 3-D, long before they are born. We can map their growth and their faces and render them in high-definition. We can listen to their hearts, examine their fingernails, and watch their noses develop. We can witness them excitedly responding to their mother's voice. And, if they are born prematurely, we can keep them alive earlier and earlier. The scientific advances have been remarkable. We might realistically hope that public opinion will follow them.

GAY MARRIAGE: THE WRONG FIGHT

All told, the debate over gay marriage is the polar opposite of the debate over abortion. The best argument in favor of extending marriage to same-sex couples is that the people wish to amend how the state defines matrimony and that governments are able to indulge that desire. Likewise, the best argument *against* extending marriage to same-sex couples is that the people don't wish to amend how the state defines matrimony and that governments are able to indulge that desire. Really, the issue is not much more complicated than that.

Attempts to turn the question into one of fundamental principle typically prove risible. In 2013, the British actor Jeremy Irons appeared on an episode of *HuffPost Live* and wondered aloud why, if gay marriage were to be deemed acceptable, it would not be okay for a father to "marry his son"? The host, Josh Zepps, spluttered a little and then suggested that this idea was ridiculous: first because fathers marrying sons is against the law, and second because there is a general "moral approbation" toward incestuous relationships. (Clearly, Zepps meant "*dis*approbation.") Wisely, for the sake of his career, Irons declined to push the point too hard.

Had he done so, however, he could well have observed that in many American states both of these things were true about gay marriage, too. Then he could have asked Zepps why he was in favor of it regardless, and watched while he squirmed.

Whatever he has convinced himself to be the case, Zepps is almost certainly *actually* in favor of gay marriage for the same reason that I am: because he has looked at the evidence and arrived at the conclusion that he doesn't particularly care either way and/or that there is more to be gained by including gays in the institution than by keeping them out. Given the considerable effort to which heterosexuals have gone over the last fifty years to devalue the institution in the law and in the culture at large, perhaps Zepps finds amusing the suggestion that secular marriage will be "ruined" if gays are permitted to partake. Maybe he is a fan of Andrew Sullivan's. Possibly he thinks that, unlike the religious question, which is profound, simply saying that "marriage is between a man and a woman" is a semantic game when it comes to the involvement of the state. Conceivably he believes that gays wishing to marry one another shows that marriage is important to them, rather than that they wish to destroy it. Who knows? Whatever the reason, though, it is a purely practical one—one that, as it relates to the government, is a product not of deep philosophy but of standard political preference. Unlike abortion, this is not an issue of life or death.

I do not intend to reiterate here my case for gay marriage. By now, we all know the ins and the outs. What I *do* wish to do, though, is to state for the record that conservatives would do well to recognize that their battle against the measure has been lost, and that it has been lost badly. Now it is time for some pragmatism—for the tactics of Dunkirk rather than the Alamo. It is Josh Zepps and not Jeremy Irons who is going to prevail. In the next few years, gay marriage will almost certainly be ushered in in all fifty states, and the manner in which that is achieved is going to matter a great deal indeed. Will the Right be ready, or will it continue to rail against the inevitable, thereby forgoing its place at the table?

I hope devoutly that it is the former. Regardless of which side they are on, conservatives and libertarians should currently be banding together, better to insist that reform be placed in its proper legal and philosophical context and that the more excitable advocates of change are not permitted to sacrifice deeply entrenched American principles in the excitement of their moment. Regrettably, my fellow proponents of gay marriage have an unfortunate tendency to abandon all propriety in pursuit of their ends—a tendency that, I would suggest, is far more dangerous to the integrity of the republic than extending marriage to gays could ever be. Resisting their excesses is imperative.

First and foremost, conservatives should vehemently reject the notion that there is any right to marriage contained within the text of the United States Constitution. The Constitution, remember, is not a synonym for "nice thing," but a codified set of rules and laws. Antonin Scalia, who wrote a blistering dissent to the opinion that struck down the Defense of Marriage Act and led, inexorably, to a host of state laws being overturned, rejected the idea that the issue is any of the court's business, mocked the notion that the framers of the Fourteenth Amendment had any such thing in mind, and contended that the decision served to "[aggrandize] the power of the court to pronounce the law" and to undermine the "power of our people to govern themselves." Further, he presciently predicted, the decision "arms well every challenger to a state law restricting marriage to its traditional definition." Since those words were written, lower courts have gutted state constitutions, often on the most frivolous of pretexts. "It is one thing for a society to elect change," Scalia concluded, but "it is another for a court of law to impose change by adjudging those who oppose it *hostes humani generis*, enemies of the human race."

Scalia is correct, and conservatives—including those such as myself who wish firmly that each state would permit gays to marry—should be deeply uncomfortable with the matter being taken away from the group to which it belongs, the voters; and vexed, too, by the invention of constitutional rights that are clearly not contained within the charter. In order to ensure the integrity of the law, champions of the existing order must remind the public that we are dealing here with a public policy change of precisely the sort that the Founders left to the discretion of the people, and not with a long-dormant provision in a malleable and evolving Constitution that is wholly silent on the matter. Unless constitutionalists wish to get themselves into trouble further down the road, they should continue to press this point, reminding the public at every turn that it is entirely possible to be in favor of gay marriage without losing one's mind.

Second, conservatives should insist vehemently that those who oppose the change are not to be ostracized, either by society or by the state—not, that is, to be rendered *hostes humani generis*. By and large, the opponents of reformulation are not "bigots" who need to be beaten down and excommunicated, but skeptics who are understandably nervous about what is a radical—and in many cases *hasty*—alteration to the social order. Republics such as the United States may reinvent their institutions and redraw their laws if they so wish. Sometimes it is necessary for them to do so. But they are under no obligation to, nor are we compelled to take seriously those who pretend that dissent is necessarily indicative of narrow-mindedness or of diseased and hateful minds. As the inimitable David Burge—better known on Twitter by the handle "Iowahawk"—argued recently, the snippy manner in which the advocates of gay marriage have gone about their crusade is repugnant. "It's hard to take a 'human rights activist' seriously," Burge wrote in 2013,

> *while he's beating someone over the head with a "NOH8" placard for holding the same position Barack Obama held until 5 minutes ago.*
>
> *So yeah, in a secular society maybe it's time for opponents to recognize a rational basis for legal SSM. But it's also time for supporters to recognize they are espousing a position that every society in the first 99.99% of human history would have considered nuts.*

Third, conservatives should refrain from reacting to the change by seeking to "get government out of marriage." Perhaps the most outspoken advocate of this approach is Senator Rand Paul, who told *National Review* in 2013 that he personally believes "in the historic and religious definition of marriage" but considers nonetheless that the law of contract can handle the question without the need for the involvement of the state. "I'm not for eliminating contracts between adults," Paul said. "I think there are ways to make the tax code more neutral, so it doesn't mention marriage. Then we don't have to redefine what marriage is; we just don't have marriage in the tax code."

Steven Greenhut, a writer at *Reason*, has offered a similar argument.

> *Marriage is primarily a pact between two people and, in the view of many, a sacrament of the church. The state merely recognizes this contract. If, say, a totalitarian government (think the Khmer Rouge or others like them that have meddled in such things) dissolved my marriage, my wife and I would still be married. The state could make our lives miserable, but it couldn't end our marriage.*

Attractive as this may sound—primarily as a useful, if churlish, way of circumventing the issue—it makes little sense on closer inspection. Greenhut is absolutely correct to say that the state's capriciously changing the definition of marriage does not alter much in the eyes of the church or of any private organization that sanctioned it. Nor, in most cases, can the reluctance of authorities to acknowledge a union drive couples apart. Nevertheless the refusal of the government to endorse one's nuptials can do some serious damage to what they mean in the real world—which, of course, is precisely why the government's endorsement is sought by gays in the first place.

As almost all libertarians acknowledge, private agreements

ultimately require *enforcing* by the state. (This in large part is why we have one.) It's all very well for us to say, "Let private contracts sort this out," but the practical benefits that those contracts confer still need the acquiescence of the government if they are to mean anything concrete. Necessarily, this raises the question of *which* contracts the state will agree to enforce and which it will decline to recognize. Not all contracts, after all, are deemed to be legitimate. I cannot enter into a legal agreement that renders me a slave; I cannot sign a covenant with a client or an employer in which I agree to work for less than the minimum wage; and I cannot agree to own property in concert with a minor. It is more or less inevitable that a significant number of the private contracts that would be designed to replace the formal institution of marriage would be deemed invalid. The government might, for example, be fine with *my* signing an agreement that made me my wife's civil partner and guaranteed joint custody of our child. The government might be fine, too, with two men doing the same thing. But would it be happy for a man to sign a series of such agreements with *multiple* women? Possibly not. And, if it would not, would its hewing to a rule that allowed straights and gays to construct contractual pseudo-marriages but excluded polygamists from doing so really be seen as less discriminatory simply because the word "marriage" isn't being used? I doubt it.

Ultimately, Greenhut and Paul are making a semantic point—and one that they do not appear to have fully comprehended. Certainly, the state could agree to stop using the word "marriage." Certainly, the state could agree to recognize and privilege a collection of contracts that approximated the institution formerly known as "marriage." Certainly, the state could claim to be indifferent as to how Americans choose to live. But whatever linguistic tricks it pulled, the government could not ultimately avoid the bigger question, which, despite our best efforts, would remain "Who may enjoy the benefits that have traditionally accrued to the married?"

Even if the United States were to move to a fully libertarian framework that relied on private contracts, the state would likely still be required to hold on to its definitions—if just to interact with the rest of the world. After DOMA was struck down in 2013, one of the first things that the federal government did was to start issuing green cards to the same-sex foreign spouses of American citizens. Why? Well, because immigration law determines that married citizens may petition for their spouses to join them in the United States, and the federal government's definition of "married" had just been changed. How, pray, would an immigration system work if the government had *no definition of marriage at all?* Would a gay couple from Sweden be allowed to immigrate together? What about a "marriage" consisting of three or more people? What about a man who married a twelve-year-old girl? Again, in all of these cases we could agree that the immigration service would not use the word "marriage" and that it would instead allow those who were bound by contracts of which it approved to apply for residency. But again, really this would change the *nomenclature*, not the system. The state would still be determining which relationships it wished to recognize and which it did not. Perhaps we would need a word to collectively describe the set of contracts that meet the standard. Might I suggest "marriage"?

Advocates of "getting the government out" note correctly that the government's issuing marriage licenses is a historical aberration. Traditionally marriages were not endorsed by the state but recognized—a regime in which the government enforced contracts that were drawn up by churches or, under the English Common Law, agreements resulting from the ongoing behavior of couples who cohabited but had never walked down the aisle. Can't we just go back to that? Hardly. For a start, while governments did tend to agree to recognize any marriage performed by a church, there was no debate as to what a marriage actually *was*. Sure, each institution might have had different rules regarding to whom it would grant a license, but the state did not have to worry about questions of category. "Marriage" was, as it had always been, a union between a man and a woman. This is no longer the case. Second, the various layers of government in the modern United States are tangled up with the institution of marriage to a startling degree. It's not just immigration. Feasibly, one could remove any mention of the word from the tax code. (Arguably, we should.) But is there the appetite to change the rules governing Medicare, Social Security, and welfare? Are government workers going to accept it if their employer suddenly refuses to extend medical benefits and life insurance to their partners on the basis that it has "gotten out of marriage"?

There are some serious questions, too, as to how useful private contracts can actually be in emulating marriage— questions that, once again, raise the possibility that by shifting to such a system we would merely be asking the government to change its language. The libertarian lawyer Doug Mataconis has asked what we would do, for example, about the principles of Tenancy by the Entirety or Spousal Testimonial Privilege, or about the "privileges that a spouse has when the others spouse dies without a will," none of which are easy to replicate via contracts.

Crucially, those who suggest a retrenchment in the area wildly underestimate the extent to which gay and lesbian couples hope to enjoy the state's imprimatur. It is no accident that Justice Kennedy's decision in the *Windsor* case spent a good deal of time discussing inclusion. DOMA should be struck down, Kennedy argued, because it

> *undermines both the public and private significance of state-sanctioned same-sex marriages; for it tells those couples, and all the world, that their otherwise valid marriages are unworthy of federal recognition. This places same-sex couples in an unstable position of being in a second-tier marriage. The differentiation demeans the couple, whose moral and sexual choices the Constitution protects and whose relationship the State has sought to dignify. And it humiliates tens of thousands of children now being raised by same-sex couples. The law in question makes it even more difficult for the children to understand the integrity and closeness of their own family and its concord with other families in their community and in their daily lives.*

In other words, it is not good enough for most gay people that their relationship be legally equal to those of straight people. Instead, they wish to be actively *approved* of. Instead, according to Kennedy, they wish to see the state "dignify" their marriage. Should it do so? For government, this is an inherently subjective question. But it is impossible to get away from the fact that, ultimately, we are deciding that we wish to extend the definition of marriage *because there is a significant demand for us to do so.* Whatever we might hear from the courts or from the opinions of our self-appointed arbiters of taste, there really is no hard-and-fast equation that makes this the "right" or "wrong" choice. It is a wholly democratic question that, at its root, comes down to "Those people wish to have their relationship recognized; will you let them?" We now live in a country in which the majority says, "Yes." Little good can come from the government's active suppression of a social change that arose organically and over the course of decades. Conservatives, who respect the complex nature of changes like these, should spend their time on more fruitful endeavors.

THE REAL THREAT

Rather than stand on the sidelines shouting "No!" conservatives should be facing down the very real threats that the partisans of gay marriage are now posing to individual liberty. Worryingly swiftly, the debate has shifted from whether gay marriage is a good idea *at all* to whether it is acceptable for anybody who opposes it to hold down a job or to be received in polite society. Of late, we have seen agitators claim the scalp of the CEO of Mozilla, Brendan Eich, who was forced to resign for the high crime of having contributed to California's Proposition 8—a measure that the majority of his fellow voters supported only six years ago; we have seen some on the Left begin to wage a war against private business owners' rights of conscience; and we have seen frequent and ugly attempts to purge the public square of those who oppose its agenda. Anyone who is skeptical that there is a movement afoot to excommunicate traditionalists should ask *Duck Dynasty*'s Phil Robertson what happens when you step out of line. Or the Benham brothers. Or even Alec Baldwin! (The opprobrium that is directed at public figures for their attitudes toward this question is, as you might imagine, wholly inconsistent. Dick Cheney was in favor of gay marriage in 2004; Hillary Clinton changed her mind in 2013. Which of them do you think is held up as the civil rights hero?)

On August 22, 2013, a time at which the majority of the states maintained their traditional definitions of marriage, New Mexico's high court upheld a decision against a private business named Elane Photography. The case had been brought after the outfit's co-owner, Elaine Huguenin, had refused to photograph the nuptials of a same-sex wedding. In a majority opinion that established that businesses in New Mexico were henceforth prohibited from declining potential clients on the basis of heartfelt religious objections, the court explained that

> *in the smaller, more focused world of the marketplace, of commerce, of public accommodation, the Huguenins have to channel their conduct, not their beliefs, so as to leave space for other Americans who believe something different. That compromise is part of the glue that holds us together as a nation, the tolerance that lubricates the varied moving parts of us as a people. That sense of respect we owe others, whether or not we believe as they do, illuminates*

this country, setting it apart from the discord that af-
flicts much of the rest of the world. In short, I would say
to the Huguenins, with the utmost respect: it is the price of
citizenship.

This terrifying notion—that forced speech is "the price of citizenship"—quickly rang alarm bells among those in the legal profession. Jordan Lorence, counsel with the Alliance Defending Freedom, urged the U.S. Supreme Court to reverse the case, thereby making "it clear that no American has to abandon their constitutionally protected freedoms just to make a living. . . . No American," Lorence argued, "should be punished or put out of business simply for disagreeing with the government's opinion on a moral issue." A Rasmussen poll conducted in the immediate aftermath of the case discovered that 85 percent of Americans concurred. Here, conservatives and libertarians should find common cause—standing together to insist that there is no good reason whatsoever why the inclusion of a minority group in an ancient social institution must result in the diminishment of others' liberty. This is not a zero-sum game, and it must not be allowed to become one—however trendy or sympathetic are the litigants.

We are in difficult territory here, I accept. Given the great evils of slavery and segregation—and the more covert forms of racism that they yielded—the question of what private actors may be forced to do by the state is a historically sensitive one. The Civil Rights Act of 1964 accords the federal government the capacity to prohibit businesses from discriminating against both customers and employees on the basis of their race, color, religion, or national origin, thereby making it illegal for a private citizen to run a restaurant that turns away workers or patrons because they possess immutable characteristics that he dislikes.

What should we think of this principle? After all, if we consider it to be inviolate, then we can hardly complain when it is applied to gays, too. My view, unpopular as I am sure it is, is that the whole idea that government exists to make private discrimination illegal is deeply suspect. Heretical as this may sound, I see no solid reason why, in a free country, individuals may not do with their own businesses and property precisely as they wish. It makes absolute sense to have rules governing the conduct of the government. Voting rules, access to public facilities, enrollment in public schools, the behavior of government agencies that receive federal funds, the choices of federal departments, and access to the court system—all of these are the business of the state. Clearly, it would be unacceptable for the state to refuse to issue driver's licenses to African Americans or to charge British writers a higher tax rate or to refuse to send the police to help individuals with certain views. Not only do we all pay the taxes that fund the government, and not only do we all have to obey its laws, but we are often unable to opt out from its purview. If I want to drive a car, for example, I have no choice but to obtain a driver's license from the powers that be.

But if private property is to mean anything, we should surely recognize that a restaurant is not the same thing as the DMV and that a wedding photographer ought not to be bound by the same rules as is the IRS. The parts of the 1964 Civil Rights Act that prevent government from discriminating against the unpopular or the downtrodden are not only constitutional but necessary; the parts that apply to private institutions, on the other hand, are flagrant violations of the American way. At one point, these violations were necessary to fight a great evil. But now, in the era of outrage media? If a particular restaurant owner won't serve me because he dislikes one or more of my immutable characteristics, so what? I'll go to the restaurant next door. And then I'll tell everyone what an ass he is.

Why, anyway, would I wish to stay? It greatly perplexes me that there is any desire to force individuals to serve those they dislike in the first place. Who among us wishes to be photographed by a person who considers our behavior to be sinful and abhorrent? Who wishes to have someone at their wedding who is being forced to work against his or her will? Who wants to violate a troubled conscience? And why, ultimately, does anybody feel the need to be endorsed by private companies run by private individuals?

Inevitably, these questions bring up a crucial distinction between the ways the Right and the Left approach the world around them. While libertarians and many conservatives see the *principle* of a given law as being distinct from the outcome of the event to which that law is applied, their opponents on the Left allow no such divergence. Thus, statutes that would protect the capacity of business owners to turn away any customers they dislike are quickly labeled as "anti-gay" or "anti-black," with no regard whatsoever for the doctrines that those laws were enacted to support. This is a dangerous instinct, for we could treat *any* classically liberal rule in this manner. The First Amendment permits individuals to say extraordinarily abhorrent things. *Brandenburg v. Ohio*, the ruling that governs modern First Amendment jurisprudence, upheld the right of neo-Nazis in Ohio to march through a Jewish area in full regalia. Does this mean that the First Amendment is "anti-Jewish"? Or does it merely mean that it doesn't allow the government to prohibit individuals from being anti-Jewish? Clearly, it is the latter. Why do we not make the same distinction when private property is involved?

Now, turning someone away from a restaurant, declining to make them a wedding cake, and refusing to take photographs of them are, by their nature, different than berating somebody in print or marching through their neighborhood dressed as a storm trooper. The former are actions; the other merely speech. But in neither case is the victim having his or her "rights" violated—at least not unless we radically alter how "rights" has been used for almost all of Anglo-American history. The only "freedom" at stake here is that of the *business owner*. Because one has no "liberty" to go into someone else's business—or, for that matter, to work there—then one cannot be denied his "rights" if that business owner decides not to serve him. Would a business owner who chose not to serve blacks or women or people with English accents prove himself to be reprehensible? Yes, of course he would. Would I go out of my way to draw attention to his behavior and encourage the free market to punish him for his actions? That depends. Sometimes this power can be used for good (say, for the boycott of a café that refuses to serve black customers). Sometimes this power can be used for ill (say, for the firing of employees who are dismissed for holding private views that have nothing to do with their job). Either way, that is a separate question.

As a rule, the Right recognizes that endorsing the right to do something is a separate thing from endorsing how that right is used; as a rule, the Left does not. In the course of my time at *National Review*, I have criticized the British government for prosecuting five Muslims who distributed material slamming gays, for jailing a young man who sent racist tweets to a professional soccer player, and for arresting a lay preacher who was arrested after he read aloud part of the Old Testament on the street. In America, I have defended a video gamer who was put in jail for making a joke about shooting up a school. On each occasion, I have been unpleasantly surprised to see people accusing me of "defending" what they *said*. Not once have I done such a thing—and nor would I. All I have asked is that the state leave the offender alone and refrain from playing arbiter of taste. Likewise, when I suggest that wedding photographers or cake makers should be left alone to make their own decisions, I am by no means endorsing those decisions: I am merely arguing that they are theirs to make and that it is better for society to figure these questions out for itself. I see nothing special about the gay marriage question that should exempt it from this rule.

NO EASY TASK

A word of caution, perhaps, for would-be social reformers. The assumption that there are hordes of fiscally conservative and constitutionally minded young people who would vote Republican if only the right "socially liberal, fiscally conservative" candidate would come along is suspect, to say the least. Since 1972, Republican presidential candidates have won the youth vote only *twice*—in 1984 and 1988—and if current trends continue, they are unlikely to add a third victory anytime soon. In the year 2000, Pew Research records, "party affiliation was split nearly evenly among the young"; by 2008, when Barack Obama ran for president, there was a *19-point gap* in favor of the Democrats. That year, Obama won 66 percent of the youth vote. Four years later—amid widespread disillusionment, and with many of those 18- to 29-year-olds now describing themselves as being "independent"—he still managed to win 60 percent. Things, let's say, are not going the GOP's way with the kids.

The recent Democratic swing is in part the product of demographic change. Young people are becoming less white, and presently nonwhites overwhelmingly vote for Democrats. But it is also a matter of general political preferences. Millennials may well have soured on President Obama personally, and on his health care reform in particular, but on a majority of non-social issues, young people still seem to be lining up on the Left. According to Pew, 31 percent of Millennials identify as "liberal," 39 percent as "moderate," and 26 percent as "conservative"—making them the only age group in which self-identified conservatives do not dominate. Worse, 53 percent of those between the age of 18 and 29 claim to want "a bigger government providing more services—the highest of any generation." Unlike every other age group, they want a government that benefits them as much as they want a government that benefits the elderly and the infirm. How committed to the welfare state are young voters? While half of them believe that, at the current rate, they will never see a dime from Social Security, a remarkable 60 percent do not want to see any cuts. Hidden Republicans these are almost certainly not!

Given all of this, two important questions come to mind. The first: How realistic is a swift Republican rebrand? The truth is that, even if the GOP changed its stripes overnight, it would have a lot of work to do to convince certain voters that it is on their side. Not only is the Democratic Party unlikely to lose its reputation as the party of social reform anytime soon, it will almost certainly fight tooth and nail to preserve its position as the party that forgives. Put bluntly, the claim that Republicans are antediluvian on matters of sex and sexuality is such a wildly profitable theme for Democrats that they will be unlikely to relinquish the fight *whatever* the GOP does. As we have seen with the wholly mendacious "War on Women" narrative on which the Left has recently settled, truth comes second to efficacy in the campaign office. Politics is a zero-sum game—that is, what is electorally profitable for Republicans is electorally *challenging* for Democrats. Are we really to believe that if Republicans effectively became Democrats on a host of questions, Democrats would suddenly welcome them into the fold?

One suspects not. Rather, as soon as Republicans had announced that they were backing away from, say, the gay-marriage issue, the Democratic Party would hit them for not being *in favor enough*: for not wanting to force photographers or cake makers to participate in weddings or for believing that the Constitution is silent on the question of "marriage equality." And if these were not available avenues, there would be something else, as there always is. As my *National Review* colleague Kevin Williamson argues, Republicans are always going to be at a disadvantage on these questions, because libertarianism and liberalism are not the same thing. Wiliamson writes that

> *"liberal" and "libertarian" come from the same linguistic root, meaning "liberty," and many libertarians will describe themselves among friends as "classical liberals"—political heirs to the Whigs and the Manchester free-traders. But "socially liberal" and "socially libertarian" today mean almost precisely opposite things. If there is one thing our "social liberals" hate, it is liberty. In their view, you're free to do as they please. . . .*
>
> *On the subject of gay marriage, they do not want a skeptical federalist—they want a president who is categorically in favor of gay marriage. They do not want somebody tolerant, but somebody committed, and willing to use the federal government to make their own preferences national policy. They don't want marriage written out of the federal tax code—they want gay marriage written into it. They demand a pro-gay president even if, like Barack Obama in 2008 and 2010 and half of 2012, he claims to be against gay marriage for reasons of cynical political self-interest. Liberalism is a subculture; they know their own. Rand Paul isn't one of them—and probably won't get their votes. In fact, whether it is abortion, guns, public-school curricula or the all-important issue of dropping the federal civil-rights hammer on nonconformist bakers, Paul can count on bitter, unified opposition from liberal social-issue voters.*

The bottom line: Any conservative-leaning "socially liberal" candidate is going to continue to have his work cut out unless he can sell his position as part of a more general philosophy of live and let live.

The second question is "At what cost to their existing base would any such transformation come?" Contemporary discussions of social issues tend to ignore that there are a significant number of Americans who identify as "conservatives" and vote for Republican candidates *precisely because* the party holds conservative social views. Long-term, on the questions of marijuana and gay marriage at least, the Republican Party will have no choice but to change. But what about now? After all, there is no guarantee that Republicans would retain their existing coalition were they to move away from these issues. In the interim, the GOP could do worse than to recognize that it is in no position for wholesale ideological purity. There are more important battles than gay marriage, including one that the Right is winning: abortion. There are few Americans who are pro-choice, opposed to marijuana legalization, and against gay marriage, which puts Republicans considering playing up the pro-life position and taking a backseat on the marriage and the marijuana questions in a rare position of strength. A candidate that can stand on a platform of leaving marijuana to the states, opposing judicial interference (but not gay marriage *per se*), and taking a hard line against the wanton murder of babies would not be in too precarious a position come election time. Not bad at all, for a party that has "lost" on social issues.

9

FOREIGN POLICY

———

So they go on in strange paradox, decided only to be undecided, resolved to
be irresolute, adamant for drift, solid for
fluidity, all-powerful to be impotent.

—**Winston Churchill,** 1936,
discussing the British government's
incoherent policy toward an
increasingly belligerent Germany

AMERICAN foreign policy is a hot mess—
directionless, weak, and irrational. As I write,
critics of the status quo are pointing to the resurgence of Islamic extremism in Iraq and beyond,
which has occurred despite assurances from
the White House that the threats were "on the
run"; to the failure of the federal government
to have established a successful status of forces
agreement in Iraq or to have left enough of a
presence there to maintain the stability of that

country; to an unpredictable style of leadership that has left observers wondering if America really means what it says; to the disastrous Russian "reset," which has yielded little more than an empowered Vladimir Putin and a resurgent Russian Empire; to the abandoning of key American allies in Europe; to a cold stance toward Israel, which is routinely told little more than that it should practice "restraint"; and to a generally unclear policy toward Iran and its nuclear program.

Conservatives tend to blame President Obama for this predicament, and they have good reason to do so. Obama has never been much interested in foreign affairs, nor has he been especially jealous of America's status as the leader of the free world. Primarily, our 44th president views the realm of foreign policy as a means by which he might distinguish himself from his political enemies, and not as one of the president's most solemn, important responsibilities.

During his 2008 primary campaign, Obama used the wars in Iraq and Afghanistan to separate himself not only from the increasingly unpopular President Bush but also from competitors within his own party, recruiting popular dissatisfaction with America's foreign wars against Hillary Clinton (who at the time was the ostensibly inevitable nominee). As Zane Albayati noted recently in *The National Interest*, in 2008,

> *the Democratic primary electorate . . . was incredulous at best of Clinton's election year conversion into an anti–Iraq War crusader. Clinton lost the nomination because of her vote to give President Bush the authorization to use force in Iraq. Obama won the nomination, and subsequently the presidency, largely because of that same vote.*

As we now know, Clinton had fatally underestimated the extent to which the Democratic Party's base had shifted on the question of foreign intervention. Obama, displaying a genius for campaigning, tapped into that sentiment brilliantly.

Or did he? The last six years would suggest that, on the question of national defense, Obama was not just posturing for the campaign trail. To all appearances, our president's interest in foreign affairs really *is* limited to ensuring that the world stage does not distract him from his ambitious domestic agenda. Casting himself as the hero who would part the seas and bring peace to a war-torn world, Obama may have paid lip service to the notion of a new American policy, but at root, he doesn't seem especially to have minded what form it took. Ultimately, his foreign policy has proven no more sophisticated than was his electioneering. "Hope and change," Americans were told, would renew the country at home and abroad and restore its standing in the world. And that was pretty much that.

Robert Gates, a veteran of the Defense Department who has served six presidents, wrote in 2013 that Obama's indifference toward the situation in Afghanistan shocked him to his core. "The president doesn't trust his commander, can't stand [Hamid] Karzai, doesn't believe in his own strategy and doesn't consider the war to be his," Gates recalled. "For him, it's all about getting out." Gates also reported being appalled to hear both Hillary Clinton and Barack Obama admit in his presence that their public opposition to the Iraq surge—which Gates oversaw—had been motivated not by sober policy calculation but by the impending Iowa caucuses.

Really, one wonders why Gates was surprised. Beyond

a general desire to remain popular—and to win the respect of the anti-American Left—Barack Obama has managed to articulate no positive foreign policy goals or clear objectives for his tenure. He stands, he explains, against "conventional thinking in Washington" and for "diplomacy"—both admirable goals in and of themselves, but useless absent a wider philosophy. As Otto von Bismarck once quipped, "diplomacy without force is like music without instruments": at some point, if it is to mean anything, you have to be prepared to play. Or, as a nervous *Economist* editorial asked in 2014, in the age of Obama "What would America fight for?" Nobody seems quite to know.

For this, one cannot blame the president alone. America's executive does not exist in a vacuum, and his actions—and indeed, *in*actions—are tied inextricably to the will of the electorate. In 2014, Ed Luce of the *Financial Times* lamented that, under Obama's leadership, the United States "is behaving like a declining hegemon: unwilling to share power, yet unable to impose outcomes." Perhaps so. But does the American public really care? When President Obama complains bitterly about those who "would go headlong into a bunch of military adventures that the American people [have] no interest in participating in," is he not speaking for the majority? When he asks with irritation, "Why is it that everybody is so eager to use military force after we've just gone through a decade of war at enormous costs to our troops and to our budget?" is he not tapping into a sentiment that the public shares? When he claims that his policy is to avoid doing anything "stupid," is he not inviting weary heads to nod in acquiescence?

If the public were truly disquieted by the country's relative disengagement—and, therefore, if voters coveted a president who was active in foreign affairs—our present situation would likely be substantially different. For better or for worse, the adventure in Iraq appears to have had the same effect on the American psyche as did Vietnam and the First World War before it: that is, to have made Americans apprehensive about military action abroad and, in consequence, about the size of the military, about the use of violence in general, and about the role that the United States should play in the world. Across the board, polling shows that the number of Americans who want their country to back off is at a twenty-year high. In 2013, Pew Research discovered that a startling 53 percent of Americans agreed with the proposition that the U.S. "should mind its own business internationally." In 1995, that number was 41 percent. In 1964, it was just 20 percent. The post-Iraq era is the first since polling began in which retrenchment represents the dominant preference of the voting public. That matters.

In 2012, the Center for Public Integrity's R. Jeffrey Smith discovered broad support for defense cuts, too, recording that "the public wants $103.5 billion in defense budget cuts, or 18 percent of the current budget; Republicans want $74 billion cut, on average, Democrats want a $124.4 billion cut, and independents want a $112.2 billion reduction."

The instinct is more bipartisan than we are led to believe. As much as anything else, Rand Paul's pronounced position within the Republican firmament is explained by his willingness to challenge conservatives' reflexive attachment to the military. In 2013, when President Obama made his erratic case for intervention in Syria, the traditional anti-war movement gained an unlikely ally: the Tea Party. "There's across-the-board opposition by Virginia Tea Party members of any U.S. involvement in Syria," Mark Daugherty, former chairman of the Virginia Tea Party Patriots Federation, told the *New York Times*. "We feel we have a basket of problems that need to be solved domestically in the U.S." Matt Kibbe, the president and CEO of the influential Tea Party group FreedomWorks, concurred, suggesting that he hadn't "seen grass-roots response this huge since that first opposition to TARP. . . . You can't get to a balanced budget," Kibbe suggested, "without putting everything on the table." Come 2016, it is not only possible but *likely* that the Republican Party will be holding primary debates in which a wide range of foreign policy positions are on offer. For the first time since the days of Robert Taft, the GOP has a neutralist wing.

For conservatives, this presents both an opportunity and a challenge. That there is a contingent on the Right that is hostile to the heady interventionism of the Bush years is a healthy thing indeed. That there is a tendency to extend this skepticism beyond prudence and into all-out disengagement, however, is rather worrying. Much as it would be nice to set American policy without reference to the harsh realities of the global environment, it is an immutable fact that we no longer live in the year 1876. And while the United States could certainly benefit from a small amount of introspection, it does not have the luxury of indulging itself for too long.

Here we would perhaps profit from a brief look at the country's history, for, as ever, there is nothing new under the sun.

"THE MISCHIEFS OF FOREIGN INTRIGUE"

The comedian Stephen Colbert once joked that "if our Founding Fathers wanted us to care about the rest of the world, they wouldn't have declared their independence from it." As with most such jibes, there is an element of truth to this. Far from being a recent aberration, confusion as to the role this country should play in the world is a long-standing American tradition. The United States is a nation that was populated by people who wished to get away from their own lands and forged by revolutionaries who had consciously rejected many of the assumptions of the Old World. It should not be a surprise that it has, at many points in its history, elected to withdraw from the strife happening abroad.

Most people alive today have not known an America that was not a superpower. But between the time the British colonists left with their tails between their legs and the Allied forces emerged victorious from the carnage of the Second World War, the United States was a radically different animal.

For the most part, this was by design. In his Farewell Address of 1796, George Washington warned gravely that "foreign influence is one of the most baneful foes of republican government," liable not merely to interrupt the "peace" and, "perhaps the liberty, of nations," but to do so under "the impostures of pretended patriotism." Washington was not advocating wholesale isolationism, making it abundantly clear that he wished devoutly to extend "commercial relations" to all and sundry. But, he averred, Americans should exhibit a steadfast aversion to "the mischiefs of foreign intrigue." This idea was not reserved solely to his faction. Thomas Jefferson, whose vision for the United States differed so considerably from Washington's that he resigned from Washington's cabinet two years into his first term, struck a similar note upon taking office in 1801, announcing in his first inaugural pitch that he hoped America would enjoy "peace, commerce, and honest friendship with all nations," but "entangling alliances with none." (That this quotation is so commonly misattributed to Washington goes some way to illustrating just how close their positions were.)

The ideal held. John Quincy Adams—whose father, John, kept the United States out of a war between Britain and France and considered this to have been the greatest achievement of his remarkable life—took these early instructions to heart, arguing in 1821 that America's gift to the world was its *values* and not its military presence. In a now famous phrase, Adams urged his countrymen to ensure that the new nation "goes not abroad, in search of monsters to destroy." For almost a century and a quarter, the country obliged him. At the height of the Civil War, Lincoln's fiery secretary of state, William Seward, intimated that despite the precarious position in which the new country found itself, he would be "defending our policy of non-intervention—straight, absolute, and peculiar as it may seem to other nations." Even a confident American victory in the First World War did little to reverse the tendency. So appalled were lawmakers by the butchery of the trenches that the United States refused to join the League of Nations, effectively closed its borders to immigration, and instituted protective tariffs to keep foreign products out. Voters, who had been surprised and horrified by the casualties sustained by the country's meager armed forces, came to believe that the war had been less of a mistake and more of a trap set by monied interests who had stirred up bellicose sentiment in order to profit financially.

This is an instinct that resurfaces in times of trouble. In 1972, with the war in Vietnam beginning to wind down, the Democratic Party's presidential candidate, George McGovern, ran on the blunt slogan "Come home, America!" He lost in a landslide, winning only Massachusetts. But his central complaint, that he was "fed up to the ears with old men dreaming up wars for young men to die in," resonated with the young, who played a crucial role in securing the nomination for him and voted for him in droves. Later, Bill Clinton would greet the end of the Cold War with the announcement of a "peace dividend" and Barack Obama would tap into public exhaustion with the wars in Iraq and Afghanistan by promising to do some "nation building at home," both men demonstrating, for those who might doubt it, that the admirable and deep-seated American traditions of isolationism and noninterventionism have not been entirely extirpated from the national character.

Even the one consistent exception to the rule—the Monroe Doctrine—does not represent a break from the noninterventionist ideal so much as a logical extension of it, representing a willingness on the part of the United States to engage in its own neighborhood, preserving its autonomy against those who might undermine it but refusing to intervene elsewhere. Making this formula explicit in 1823, Monroe asserted

> *as a principle in which the rights and interests of the United States are involved, that the American continents, by the free and independent condition which they have assumed and maintain, are henceforth not to be considered as subjects for future colonization by any European powers.*

This reservation has obtained ever since. For much of their history, Americans have been eager to leave the Old World behind them. Many of them, it seems, still are.

IF NOT AMERICA, WHO?

As attractive and successful as the noninterventionist instinct has been at various points in the nation's past, it did not arise—or survive—in a vacuum. Between its resounding victory at Waterloo in 1815 and the end of the Second World War in 1945, the British Empire quite literally "ruled the waves." Projecting a naval force that could not be matched by any other power and controlling almost all of the world's maritime trade routes, the British not only ensured relative global stability but accommodated and gave teeth to the untrammeled commerce so dearly valued by Washington and his acolytes, abolished slavery and took a lead in upholding the classically liberal values of individual freedom, and ensured that no other nation could rise to become their equal. There was just one global hegemon—Britain—and the United States was fortunate that it shared so many of its values and its aims. "We think in English," Alexander Hamilton told the British envoy George Beckwith after the Revolution, "and have a similarity of prejudices, and of predilections." Britain would go on to back the Monroe Doctrine.

The British emerged victorious from World War II. But they also emerged broke and broken, on the edge of losing much that they had held dear. In concert with the Allied forces, Churchill had succeeded in saving his "island home" and crushing the existential threat that fascism presented. (The threat from communism, fascism's cousin on the Left, was just beginning.) What he had not done, however, was ensure that the British Empire lasted "for a thousand years." Having helped to save the mother country once again, Britain's imperial possessions were growing in confidence, and some sought to go out on their own. Britain had neither the treasure nor the will to prevent them. Imperial administrators, recognizing the dire straits in which the mainland and the Empire found themselves, had little choice but to hand over the baton.

Almost overnight, the United States was forced to adapt to the reality of its being not merely *a* global player but now *the* global player—the standard-bearer for the free West and the first line of defense against the march of global communism. For many in the American establishment, this shift was welcomed. For others, it was regarded as a burden. ("Uneasy," Shakepeare wrote, "lies the head that wears a crown.") Regardless, the baptism had taken place. Isolationism, non-interventionism, minding your own business—whatever you want to call these things—were one thing when someone else was guaranteeing the peace. But they represented a luxury that the United States could no longer afford now that the country was responsible for keeping the global order.

The "before" and "after" pictures are startling. Between 1800 and 1940, federal spending on defense hovered around 1 percent of GDP, exceeding 2 percent only in times of declared war. Since 1940, by contrast, defense spending has never dropped below 3.6 percent of GDP and has averaged between 5 and 10 percent. The standing army—an idea that was in principle abhorrent to the Founders and in practice unrealistic during most of the republic's history—became an unquestioned feature of American life. In 1939, as Hitler prepared to take over Europe, the U.S. military ranked 17th in the world, with just over 200,000 soldiers in the regular army and just under 200,000 members of the National Guard. By 1950, the army numbered 1.5 million. The size of the military reached 3 million in 1970, and it has fluctuated considerably since then, but never dropped below 1.5 million.

Without having entirely asked for the change, the United States has thus found itself in a position of great power and responsibility. Is this a good thing? That depends, of course, on how one sees the world. As with all such questions, the first line of inquiry must be: "As opposed to *what?*" As a purely abstract matter, it is easy to venture that one does not like the cost of the American military, or that one is uncomfortable with the amount of power that the United States enjoys in the world, or that one considers the martial values that inevitably creep in when nations take a leading role in international affairs to be destructive to liberty. But it is much more difficult to answer the question of what we might do instead.

Given the longevity of British-American power, it is tempting to imagine that international affairs exist naturally in their current state: that, as a matter of course, the seas are open, global trade is protected, and the worst instincts of anti-Western actors are kept in check. Sadly, this is not the case. Were the United States to disengage from the world in a serious way, someone else would almost certainly step in to fill the void. Would we like them? Almost certainly not. Who, I like to ask anybody who gripes about American "hegemony," would you wish to see instead? China? Russia? *France?* And which of our previous adversaries do you wish were still around to balance out America? The Soviet Union? The Ottoman Empire? The Romans?

Senator Marco Rubio, who despite his Tea Party roots has been a consistent voice in favor of American power since his election to the Senate in 2010, likes to remind conservatives that, if they "think high taxes and regulations are bad for our economy," they should wait until they see "global instability and the spread of totalitarianism." Rubio frequently taps into a long-standing conservative belief—often coined lazily as "peace through strength"—that a world with a thriving system of free trade, free movement, and peaceful cooperation requires a dominant liberal power: a country that, for its own benefit and for the benefit of the wider world, is prepared to act as the supplier of stability. It is not enough, conservatives contend, for the world merely to enjoy liberal institutions such as the U.N., the World Bank, or international markets; there has to be a single force that backs them up.

"A world without U.S. primacy," the political scientist Samuel Huntington wrote in 1993,

> *will be a world with more violence and disorder and less democracy and economic growth than a world where the*

United States continues to have more influence than any other country in shaping global affairs. The sustained international primacy of the United States is central to the welfare and security of Americans and to the future of freedom, democracy, open economies, and international order in the world.

Note, if you will, what he does *not* say. He does *not* say that the United States necessarily needs to invade particular countries or to start wars of preemption. He does *not* say that American soldiers need to go chasing after all bad actors or to intervene against each and every atrocity. He does *not* suggest that American blood and treasure should be expended in the pursuit of nation building. In fact, he doesn't endorse any particular actions *at all.* But he *does* say that the United States should "have more influence than any other country in shaping global affairs."

This distinction is crucial. There is a significant difference between, say, opposing the decision of the United States to go into Iraq in 2002 and wishing for the United States to draw back from the world stage anytime a crisis arises. It is entirely feasible for America to lead without needing to rush to the scene of every fire in every corner of the world. It is possible to observe that the instincts of the current administration are disastrous for the global order without finding the need to go back to the Bush Doctrine. Not every intervention is Iraq.

This is a reality that the Obama administration is keen to obfuscate. In a speech at West Point in 2014, the president sought to imply that there were two basic American approaches to international affairs: disengagement or all-out war. This is demonstrably false and the attempt earned him scorn and animadversion in even the traditionally friendly pages of the *New York Times* and the *Washington Post*. The United States has a broad array of ways in which it can project power—all of which cost money but not of all of which require frequent and costly intervention, the launching of land wars, or the quixotic attempt to change other nations from the inside. The most basic is by ensuring that it has a bigger military than does any other nation, and that other countries believe that, if it needs to, it will use it. Another is to do just that—putting out small fires before they become bigger ones; moving military equipment around the world, either to keep open the lanes of commerce and communication or to dissuade other powers from acting on their worst instincts; conducting limited bombing raids against selected targets; and sending resources and weapons to allies and partners.

In a time of ostensible peace, it can be tempting to regard military spending as being inherently wasteful. Especially during a recession, the complaint that the United States is spending trillions on a fighting force that never actually does anything—or at least that will never be used to anywhere near its capacity—is an alluring one. But it is also rather misleading, akin in its puerility to the notion that America ought to repeal the Second Amendment because the country has not yet become tyrannical. Advocates of unmatched American military power believe that the global order is secure and America is untouched precisely *because* it has a stronger military than everybody else—and, yes, because it sometimes intervenes. They believe that the reason America has not been involved in a third world war is that it would be folly for anyone else to start one—or even to provoke the United States. And they believe that if an irrational actor were to do the unthinkable, America, and those who would depend upon her response, would benefit from physical preparedness and not lofty rhetoric.

Trying to pin down the complex causes of the Second World War is the work of a lifetime. One thing, though, is absolutely clear: It was *not* caused because free countries were too strong or too resolute. On the contrary, the world's former hegemon—the British Empire—elected in the period following the horrors of the trenches to disarm itself and thus to allow the rise of smaller powers that, checked early, would have been unable to plunge the world into chaos. The United States simply has to avoid this course. The great virtue of unmatched American power is that it serves as an insurance policy, preventing problems from occurring in the first place and guaranteeing that, if things ever were to go disastrously wrong, Western democracy would have a fighting chance. It is impossible to know exactly how many soldiers would have been saved in the twentieth century had there been no vacuum into which bad actors could surge, but we can be sure that it would be in the millions. Have we learned nothing? Watching this president abdicate his responsibilities—sometimes to the applause of large sections of the Right—one is tempted to wonder.

Rather than questioning America's role in the world, reformers within the conservative movement would do better to put their criticism to more moderate and constructive use. Just as crucial as ensuring that the United States does not mistake the keeping of order for nation building is ensuring that the military is not permitted to get away with a carte blanche approach to spending and management that would be humored in no other part of the government. Pro-military conservatives who simultaneously agitate for small government and substantial defense spending are sometimes characterized as being hypocrites, the typical taunt being that the Right likes federal spending and centrally directed organizations when it suits them. This, I think, is a silly brief. By its very nature, the military is unique, and its advocates are correct to note that it is by far the most important of all the functions that the federal government performs, not simply because the United States serves as the linchpin of the global order but because— philosophically and constitutionally—defending the realm is the primary reason that the federal government exists *in the first place*. Where one can make a compelling case for the distribution of welfare at the local and state levels—or, indeed, through nongovernmental institutions such as charities and churches—one will struggle to assemble an argument against a single, national, government-run military. We could take substantial strides toward a more robust federal system, and we would still end up with one, and not fifty, armies.

Nevertheless, that the military should be privileged does not mean that it should be indulged, nor that we should accept with alacrity the inefficiency and special favors to which all state-run enterprises inevitably tend. Any federal budget that is assembled from scratch will rightfully feature defense as the first expenditure, yes—before health care, education, pensions, food stamps, and all other palliative outlays. But this does not require that it be accorded a blank check. One of the Left's greatest political tricks is to have conflated in the minds of the general public the ends and the means—in other words, to have shaped a political zeitgeist in which believing in a given mission means endorsing all that is done in its execution. This is how the execrable teachers' unions have got away for so long with pushing destructive and naked self-interest in the name of "the children." This is how the IRS manages to respond to reports of its corruption and incompetence with a call for increased funding. This, too, is how a remarkable reduction in the number of Americans who work on farms has been met with a remarkable *increase* in the number of Americans who work for the Department of Agriculture. There is really no reason why the Pentagon should be allowed to get away with the same game.

As a rule, conservatives understand these arguments well—until it comes to defense. Then they shy away from them. George Will's aforementioned jab that sequestration "forced liberals to clarify their conviction that whatever the government's size is at any moment, it is the bare minimum necessary to forestall intolerable suffering" is a funny one. But did the smaller outlays on defense that were the price of sequestration not also drive conservatives so crazy that they conspired to get rid of its cuts?

Even if the United States could do with no fewer pieces of military hardware than it currently owns, there is no reason whatsoever why the Right should not be out there railing against waste and, crucially, against military procurement being used as a means by which politicians can bring federal dollars back to their constituencies. Nor should it be evaluating military spending on any other basis than its necessity. How many jobs it creates, where those jobs are, and what cuts would do to families and local economies are irrelevant. If these arguments cannot be used to justify other make-work programs, they should not be used to justify military-based ones either.

Unfortunately, the military is blighted by the unholy combination of almost endless resources and a systemic culture of waste. Loren Thompson, a *Forbes* contributor, suggested in 2011 that

> *if you add up all the money spent on military systems that got funded but not fielded since the Cold War ended, it probably tops $100 billion. We'll never know the full amount, because some of the biggest projects are hidden in secret spy-agency accounts. Defense contractors are reflexively blamed for the waste because politicians and policymakers are even less interested in accountability than they are in precise accounting.*

Among the projects that have been paid for but cancelled in the last decade are a $2 billion mobile cannon and its $1.2 billion successor; a $7 billion reconnaissance helicopter, and its successor, too; a "Future Combat System" that was summarily axed after nearly $19 billion had been funneled into its development; a $3 billion "expeditionary fighting vehicle" that was eventually deemed surplus to requirements; and an "NPOESS" satellite system that cost taxpayers $6 billion. The Lockheed Martin VH-71 Kestrel, a new helicopter model for the President of the United States (Marine One), was scrapped after $4.4 billion had been spent on its development. Worse, the nine VH-71s that the federal government had already built when the project was scrapped were quietly sold to Canada for $164 million for use as spare parts—a 26-fold loss on investment.

Who, honestly, can be surprised? The Defense Finance and Accounting Service confirmed in a 2013 Associated Press story that, for the Pentagon and its subsidiaries, "fudging the accounts with false entries is standard operating procedure." The problem, the AP concluded, was "the Pentagon's chronic failure to keep track of its money—how much it has, how much it pays out and how much is wasted or stolen." It is endemic. The culture, Defense Secretary Robert Gates confirmed in 2010, is one of "endless money." His successor, Leon Panetta, lamented in 2011 that the Department of Defense was "the only major federal agency that cannot pass an audit today." Who is surprised that this is the result? And where were the conservative voices decrying this extravagance?

Conservatives should recognize that indulging this behavior damages their credibility as the champions of efficiency and good government, and undermines their military goals. For years, the Left has suffered from the poor quality of government services, the Right's warning that the latest progressive program would inevitably be the "DMV writ large" proving a reliable and efficacious line of attack. As long as the Right covers for the military's excess, there is no reason that this cannot be turned on them to undermine the programs they do like. Conservatives have a solid reason for prioritizing defense. The United States is invaluable in the world, and the costs of its permitting anybody to catch up with it are unimaginable. But in a time of scarce resources and political dissatisfaction with the Pentagon, the case for an unassailable force is all the more difficult to make. Pro-military conservatives have a responsibility to ensure that whatever charges the naysayers may throw, hypocrisy is not among those that will stick.

10

DEMOGRAPHICS

AND THE FUTURE

———

THE United States is welcoming of immigrants in a way that almost no other nation can match, remaining perhaps the only place on Earth where a human being can leave his home country and, within a few years, claim genuinely to be *of* the foreign society he has entered. I am not yet a citizen of the U.S., but in three years, when I have taken my oath, nobody will question me when I tell them that I am an "American." This is not because I am white or because I grew up in a Christian country or because I am fluent in the English language, but because becoming an American is more akin to becoming, say, a Catholic, than it is anything else. That is, it is an identity one takes on, not one that must be inherited. Few would presume to laugh at an

Indian immigrant who told them that he was an "an American now," nor would they be likely to question a convert from Nigeria or from Japan. On the contrary: That anybody can adopt the American identity is assumed as an article of national faith—part of what helps to make America exceptional. Were I to spend a lifetime in China, I would never be able to boast of being "Chinese," nor, in truth, would it be likely to cross my mind. That's just not how it works.

To be an "American," one primarily requires what F. Scott Fitzgerald memorably described as "a willingness of the heart." As are religious converts, newcomers to the creed are expected to agglutinate themselves to the essential conceits of the society, and to abide by its laws and canonical works—in this case, by promising fealty to the Constitution, to the principles of the Declaration of Independence, to the rule of law and to the principle of equality, and to the individual liberties that are protected by a market economy. Crucially, neophytes are expected to respect the basic structure by which their own idiosyncrasies are protected. Immigrants may retain much of themselves, of course. Indeed, they are invited to do precisely that. But they are not expected to move to the United States in order to try to make it more like the countries they forsook. Ask ten Americans on the street what they expect of the immigrant population, and you will likely invite ten instances of the same answer: "Get a job, don't become a burden, work hard, and *assimilate*." Pretty straightforward stuff.

In theory, at least, our political system acknowledges this sentiment. Recognizing that acclimatizing oneself to a new nation takes time, the federal government insists upon a considerable waiting period between an immigrant's being admitted to the country and his being given a passport; it requires a written test that ensures that would-be citizens can speak English, that they have a reasonable grasp of the relevant history, and that they are familiar with the political and philosophical tenets of the country in which they would be voting; and it marks newcomers' transitions from alien to full member of the polity with a formal ceremony, rather than with a letter or a text message. Why does it do all of these things? Because it understands that nations are filled with people, and that if the people cannot agree upon the fundamental framework under which they are to live, they will tear each other apart.

From the first days of independence, the importance of preserving the national ethos was readily apparent. In his *Notes on the State of Virginia*, Thomas Jefferson predicted that

> *we are to expect the greatest number of emigrants. They will bring with them the principles of the governments they leave, imbibed in their early youth; or, if able to throw them off, it will be in exchange for an unbounded licentiousness, passing, as is usual, from one extreme to another. It would be a miracle were they to stop precisely at the point of temperate liberty.*

Harsh as this may sound to ears that have become attuned to the witless mantra of multiculturalism, Jefferson was calling attention to a critical reality: that societies do not merely jump fully constructed out of the ground, nor can they easily be recovered when they are changed for the worse. Instead, they are the product of definite influences, strong institutions, and substantial periods of painful evolution and hard-won entrenchment. As Daniel Hannan observes in *Inventing Freedom*, we take for granted the sanctity of "elected parliaments, habeas corpus, free contract, equality before the law, open markets, an unrestricted press, the right to proselytize for any religion, jury trials," and more. But "these things are not somehow the natural condition of an advanced society." Instead, they are a miracle, representing the escape from the ugly circumstances under which most people have lived throughout human history—and continue to live today. Preserving them is our life's work.

When thinking about the question of immigration, conservatives and libertarians tend to clash—and strongly. As a rule, the conservative position is that nations are not nations unless they have borders; that culture matters enormously; that a country cannot absorb an infinite number of newcomers and expect automatically to preserve its way of life; that what protects the enormous cultural diversity and energy in the United States is the libertarian framework that permits individuals, families, and the building blocks of civil society to operate as they see fit; that in an age of international terrorism, some form of screening of travelers is imperative; and that the United States should thus have strict and tailored immigration laws that are enforced to the letter. By contrast, the libertarian position is that all individuals have a human right to relocate anywhere they wish; that almost anybody who wants to come to this country should be permitted to enter, providing that he can support himself; that it is peculiar that conservatives who do not trust the government to run much of anything would nonetheless wish the state to decide who may come in to work and live among us and who may not; and that the United States should thus not have much of an operating border at all. These two standpoints are irreconcilable.

Unlike their fellow travelers on the hard Left, libertarians do not adopt their open-borders approach because they fail to value the American experiment, because they believe that all cultures are equal, or because they cravenly hope that importing people from countries with socialist economies will aid them in their attempt to transform the United States into Europe. Nor are they opposed to the involvement of the state because they believe that expecting immigrants to assimilate to their host culture is inherently imperialistic or intolerant. Rather, they come down where they do because they have an unfortunate tendency to underestimate how sensitive the status quo really is and, critically, because they presume that the United States exists not *as it is* but *as they would like it to be.*

As I argued in Chapter 2, if libertarians have an Achilles' heel, it is that they tend to start conversations about public policy by presuming that the country already enjoys the limited government and free market economy that they covet. The immigration debate serves as no exception. Here, libertarians prefer to talk about the subject as if the United States had no welfare system; as if the scope of the federal government were in any meaningful way restricted; as if the market were permitted to operate in an unfettered manner; and as if—as it arguably did in the nineteenth century—a harsh sink-or-swim culture can be trusted to leave the question to regulate itself.

This, in my view, is a suicidal mistake. To compare the United States as it stands now to the one that existed during the immigrant waves of the late nineteenth and early twentieth centuries is, frankly, nonsensical. As Milton Friedman, a man who was reasonably friendly toward the idea of open borders, argued,

> *free immigration, in the same sense as we had it before 1914 is not possible today. Why not? Because it is one thing to have free immigration to jobs. It is another thing to have free immigration to welfare. And you cannot have both. If you have a welfare state, if you have a state in which every resident is promised a certain minimal level of income, or a minimum level of subsistence, regardless of whether he works or not, produces it or not. Then it really is an impossible thing.*

I am, of course, with the libertarians in wishing that the federal government would get out of the way. But this, for now at least, is not the country in which we live. Instead, we live with a welfare system that changes the calculation considerably.

It is not just a question of economics, but of politics, too. The data shows that immigrants vote for larger welfare systems than do native-born Americans. This, advocates insist, is not because immigrants prefer larger government *per se* but because they are disproportionately poor. This seems to be the case. But that only raises another question. This *is* a country with a welfare system that is going bankrupt, with a workforce participation rate that is at its lowest since 1978, and with a political climate in which the friends of liberty are increasingly outnumbered. Why, pray, would libertarians so much as *dream* of importing an unlimited number of people who—through no fault of their own—are likely to vote for the long-term expansion of everything they dislike? And why do they reject the conservatives' preference for bringing in a limited number and giving them time and space to blend in? I have never heard a satisfactory answer to these questions.

Nor have I been given a solid explanation as to why, as a general matter, it is illegitimate for the government of the United States to put the interests of the citizenry that it serves above the interests of the citizens of other countries. Libertarians like to accuse conservatives who wish to regulate immigration of "social engineering." But this is one of those few areas in which social engineering is a genuinely good thing! It is not the role of our elected representatives to equivocate between foreigners and American citizens, but rather to act in the name of those it represents in ensuring that the precepts on which the nation was founded are upheld. On this, conservatives should be harsh and clear: Distressing as it might be for the would-be huddled masses to acknowledge, migrants move to the United States not because they enjoy a "right" to change country but because the existing polity wishes to add them to its ranks.

I got to America partly because I have a degree from Oxford University, partly because I had a job offer from a prestigious magazine that was willing to pay me enough to keep me from becoming a public charge, and partly because the immigration system included categories that were designed to encourage the entry of people with qualifications like mine. If I had been born in Malawi, I probably wouldn't be here. Is this "unfair"? In an abstract sense, sure. There are, no doubt, many Malawians who are smarter than I am and, if given a good shot, would go on to do more impressive things. Most of them will never get the chance to come to the U.S. But, really, so what? America is a country, not a global charity. With the notable exception of those who are fleeing death and persecution—for whom the country must remain a shining city on a hill—the United States does not exist to improve the living conditions or to indulge the dreams of everybody in the world. It exists to serve its people and to guarantee their liberty.

Conservatives should focus first on making this general principle clear, and then on articulating exactly what those who are already here should want and expect from their immigration system. In my experience there is a real disconnect between the way most Americans *believe* the immigration regimen works and the way it *actually* works. Most voters, for example, do not realize that, post-1965, the system guarantees that almost nine in ten newcomers to the United States are selected not on the basis of any professional skills or personal virtues that they might possess, but because they have a family member here who is able to sponsor them. Likewise, most voters seem to be unaware that the Comprehensive Immigration Reform bill that passed the Senate in 2013 dealt with a great deal more than the problem of the border with Mexico, and would have allowed the arrival of an extra 30 million people over the next decade—almost none of whom, again, would have been selected on any other grounds than that they happened to have relatives in the country. Most Americans, too, overestimate the number of people who are granted asylum in the United States or are admitted as refugees.

Moreover, most Americans seen unaware that the influx across the southern border is breaking with a time-honored American preference for preventing social balkanization. As Kevin Williamson notes,

it is one thing to have a couple of Ukrainian churches in Philadelphia or a handful of German-speaking communities in Texas. It is another thing to have a socio-linguistic Berlin Wall or three running through practically every community in the country. Adjacency to Mexico, along with easier travel and communication, makes assimilating Mexican immigrants more difficult than assimilating the Irish generations ago. This is not at all helped by opportunistic political entrepreneurs such as La Raza and MEChA, which cultivate racial sentiment and separatism within Hispanic communities. Some parts of the country, such as my native West Texas, have long been Anglo-Hispanic cultural hybrids, and that can be a wonderful thing. It is not necessarily a good model for the country at large.

Whether this is a "wonderful thing" is for the existing polity to decide. Rarely, though, are such questions debated in public. Both libertarians and progressives have a pernicious habit of distilling what is a complex question into a single term, "immigrant," thereby failing to distinguish between the illiterate farmer from Guatemala, the Irishman who came to New York on holiday and never went back, and the Nobel Prize–winning physicist from India. Conservatives should ensure that the subtleties are not ignored, and that the broadest range of existing citizens is involved in the conversation. The future of the country depends upon it.

You will have perhaps noticed that I did not address the question of the Republican Party's share of the Hispanic vote, nor of the crisis on the southern border. This was deliberate. There is a pervasive and unlovely tendency among the pundit class to presume that conservatives are destined forever to lose the Hispanic vote unless they bow before the wishes of the Democratic Party and acquiesce in whatever magic bullet is being proposed this week. This, to put it kindly, is silly. Hispanics are not mindless automatons who think as a homogeneous bloc, nor are they subservient fools who will immediately disregard their present convictions if Republicans elect to pander to them for a few months at a time. Instead, they are a complex and diverse group—as sophisticated and as multifarious as any other. Not only do Hispanics display different political leanings depending on where they live in the country, how long their families have been here, and where they sit economically and socially, but, as the *Washington Post*'s Chris Cillizza has written, "the Latino community is only thought of as 'the Latino community' by those not in it. . . . There isn't," Cillizza writes, "a single definitional (or electoral) strain that runs through everyone who, at least according to the Census Bureau, is Hispanic."

The idea that if the Republican Party agrees to the Democrats' vision for comprehensive immigration reform they will instantaneously be back in the game is a preposterous and an offensive one, and it does not reflect well upon those who advance it. Markos Moulitsas, the firebrand editor of the *Daily Kos*, wrote in 2013 that if progressives could be patient, they would eventually see even Texas turn in their electoral favor. By 2014, Moulitsas admitted, not "enough time will have passed" for the Left "to be bailed out by demographics." But, he suggested, such a bailing out was on the way. Why? Because young people are becoming less and less white (especially so in a border state such as Texas), people who are less white tend to vote Democratic, and, in consequence, the Democratic Party will need to do little more than to sit back and wait for the nonwhites to up their numbers. This is politics by racial categorization—and it is ugly.

It is also dangerous. Because they dislike lumping individuals into generalized groups, conservatives should shy away from it on philosophical and ideological grounds. But they should also reject the presumption that what is true now will be true forever. Even if we are to treat everybody with brown skin and some connection to the Spanish language as being part of one group, the assumption that this group has glued itself permanently to the fortunes of the Democratic Party is a peculiar one. Far from representing a collection of partisan die-hards, "Hispanic" voters have demonstrated a remarkable willingness to adjust their opinions to the changing political climate. In December 2012, Obama's approval rating among Hispanics was 75 percent. By November 2013, after various scandals had reared their ugly heads and Obamacare's disastrous launch had put a dent in the president's perceived competence, that number stood at 52 percent. By July 2014, it was at 44 percent—only 3 points higher than the national average.

Obamacare, too, has fallen out of favor. Before the exchanges were launched in October 2013, Hispanic approval of the law was stable, at 61 percent. In March 2014, Pew Research confirmed, "as many Hispanics [approved] as [disapproved] (47%–47%) of the new health care law."

Pew has also poured cold water on the conceit that Hispanic voters are interested only in immigration—a false impression that is promulgated feverishly on cable news and on Capitol Hill. A June 2014 poll revealed that one in three Hispanics considers immigration to be "extremely important," while more than half were more preoccupied with "education," "jobs and the economy," and "health care." This trend has remained the same for years. "Since 2007," Pew records, "about one-third of Hispanic registered voters have called immigration an 'extremely important' issue to them personally. Even among Hispanic immigrants, the share was 35% in 2012." Moreover, a significant chunk of Hispanics actually agree with the *conservative position* on illegal immigration, around one-third endorsing the Republican Party's preference for securing the border before passing any form of amnesty or forgiveness for those here illegally. Allegedly "anti-Hispanic" ballot initiatives in California and Arizona draw roughly the same levels of support, too.

This is not, of course, to suggest that conservatives can expect to ignore the question of immigration completely and remain in good favor with Hispanic voters. Nor is it to suggest that the Republican Party cannot do itself significant harm by talking about immigration insensitively or by conflating too closely Hispanic Americans and illegal immigrants. But it *is* to observe, as *RealClearPolitics'* senior election analyst Sean

Trende has done doggedly since 2012, that we should "challenge the almost universally unchallenged argument that the only real debate is whether the GOP will die a slow death or a fast one if it doesn't back" the comprehensive immigration reform that the Democratic Party is so forcefully pushing.

To cut through the rhetoric is to see that conservatives should be internalizing two important things: First, that the arrogant sense of possession and inevitability that one sees from the likes of Markos Moulitsas is misplaced. Broadly speaking, "Hispanic" voters do not have a unique set of expectations, but tend to want the same things as do white voters. The primary reason that they vote for the Democratic Party is not that Republicans are seen as the enemy—it is that the Democratic Party is seen as being the party of the poor, and Hispanics are generally poorer than are whites. If Republicans want to turn around their performance here, their aim should be to appeal more effectively to the poor and to the middle class, and not simply to start speaking in Spanish.

Second, conservatives should recognize that they do not actually need to win "the Hispanic vote" *in toto*; they just need to win more of it than they are winning now—*and they need to do so while winning other voters*. Had Mitt Romney won as large a percentage of the Hispanic vote as George W. Bush did in 2004 (44 percent), he would still have lost the White House. Romney won 27 percent. This was a poor show, to be sure, but it was not what cost him the election. The *Washington Examiner*'s Byron York has run the numbers and calculated that in order to have defeated Obama, Romney would have needed to win *73 percent* of the Hispanic vote. This "suggests," York notes, "that Romney, and Republicans, had bigger problems than Hispanic voters." Translation: Hispanic voters are not a magic bullet, but one part of a general quandary. Going after them should not be seen as an end in and of itself. It should be seen as part of a broader project.

All of which is to say that any conservative resurgence will—and should—be a long-term enterprise and not the product of glib tweaks here and there, or of the micro-targeting of small or racially defined groups of voters. The Right should vehemently resist the temptation to chase pockets of the electorate and instead make a color-blind pitch for limited and humble government, for localism, for reform, and for the historical framework that has made this country great. As I have argued throughout this book, conservatives should be changing that pitch in a number of important ways—not in order to pander, but because they recognize that it is in the general interest of the country.

Where they can and should change their tactics is in *how* they sell their ideas. In public affairs, the manner in which something is being said can often matter as much as what is being said. Sometimes, showing up is 90 percent of the game. If conservatives wish to sell minorities on their gospel of in-dividual rights, personal responsibility, and American excep-tionalism, they will have to engage. This will be easier said than done. Fifty years ago, politics did not determine your neighbors. Some of the country's largest cities were run by Democrats, and some were run by Republicans. It was un-likely that you could tell your friends' voting preferences by the car that they drove or the books that they read. Americans associated with other Americans. Now, the country is frag-mented in a much more pronounced way. Sparsely populated rural areas are, almost without exception, run or represented by Republicans; densely populated urban centers are almost exclusively run or represented by Democrats. Never the twain shall meet.

Take a look at the electoral chart in the wake of a presidential election and you will see a sea of red with a few little blue sections to balance it out. Because, in most elections, Republican candidates are able to win solely by appealing to Republican voters, their temptation is to ignore everybody else and to craft their message purely for the base. As the demographic makeup of the country changes, this is going to become less and less viable.

Does the Right understand this? If so, it has a funny way of showing it. Frankly, there are an unforgivable number of areas in which conservatives simply don't play at all, ceding the argument to the other side without a fight and reinforcing the idea that theirs is the ideology of one section of the population and not of the country as a whole. In 2012, it was reported that vice-presidential candidate Paul Ryan had requested permission to go into America's inner cities and talk to minority groups about conservatism, but that the Romney campaign had refused permission. This is unforgivable.

When conservatives *do* try, they are far too easily cowed. Rand Paul's trip to the traditionally black Howard University was met with derision and criticism by the Left—some of it deserved, much of it not. Tim Scott, the black South Carolina senator, went undercover as a volunteer at a Goodwill store and was immediately mocked by the *Washington Post* for "anecdote shopping." When, in 2013, Paul Ryan made a substantive attempt to address the question of long-term unemployment in America's cities, he was rewarded with accusations of racism and quickly apologized for his candor.

What *should* conservatives do about this? Carry on! Carry on and expand the effort. Talk to everyone—not just around election time but *constantly*. Fight the good fight. The British socialist Roy Hattersley described with reluctant admiration how Margaret Thatcher dealt with her opponents' many attempts to beat her down. "You could fire a bazooka at her and inflict three holes," Hattersley said in 1990. "Still she kept coming." So many of us know exactly what it is like to be under fire in this way—especially when we are addressing any topic on which the Left feels vulnerable. As the libertarian writer and economist Thomas Sowell once quipped, in the modern age the definition of a "racist" is a conservative who is winning an argument. In the age of Obama, conservatives are labeled "racist" whether they are winning, losing, or holding their own; when they are up, and when they are down; when they speak and when they are silent; when they are listening and when they are not; whether the topic is related to race or whether it has nothing whatsoever to do with it. There is now an entire cable network devoted to the discussion of race and racism. I have joked, on occasion, that I would like to host my own MSNBC show titled "And Now . . . Subjects Other Than Race."

How to react? Brush it off, of course. Ignore the lot of them. Disregard the nonsense and carry on happily with the rest. Conservatives have on their side the most successful, virtuous, and *radical* political philosophy in the history of the world. Unlike their opponents, whose ideology is distressingly ahistorical and therefore liable to be shaped by the transient and fashionable demands of self-serving interest groups, conservatives have a North Star to guide them and to establish their place in history's complex sky. From time to time, they have lost track of it in the night, their boats lurching erratically toward the wrong shores, their captains and crew scrambling to make sense of the uncharted waters. But this is to be expected—perhaps, even, to be relished once in a while. Their task is to catch sight of the star once again, to work out what went wrong, and to sail on without loss of enthusiasm or purpose.

Have at it: the future is there for the taking.

Acknowledgments

I<small>N</small> the movies, writers benefit greatly from the montage, their work of days and weeks made to look romantic through energetic music and the compression of time. Real life, alas, is not like this. In the real world, writing is a solitary, slow, and often silent pursuit, during which one struggles to see the forest for the trees. Throughout this process, my wife, Kate, has been little short of a saint: patiently acting as a scribe while I walked pontificating around the living room; accepting with alacrity the series of cancelled plans and last-minute alterations to the calendar; taking in stride the frequency with which the door to my office was closed; and pretending bravely that she thinks I have a point on the War on Drugs. I owe her a much-deserved trip to Vermont.

I have also been fortunate to have worked with two superb editors at Random House: Stephanie Knapp and Derek Reed, both of whom have guided me expertly through new terrain. It is no exaggeration to say that I have learned from them how to write a book. On the publishing side, Campbell Wharton, who took over from Sean Desmond a few months into the process, has been warm and energetic and encouraging. I am thankful for his help.

I have long insisted that the greatest benefit that a good university accords to its students is the chance to surround themselves with people smarter and more educated than they. For this reason, among many others, it is my great privilege to work at a place like *National Review*. Rich Lowry and Jack Fowler both took a gamble on me when they had good no reason to do so, and they continue to do so. I am eternally grateful for their guidance and indulgence. Kevin Williamson is a friend and a mentor, and he has had a great effect on my thinking. It is no surprise, perhaps, that he is quoted in these pages more than any other. I cherish my conversations with Jay Nordlinger, one of the world's great men of letters. Patrick Brennan and I continue to spar—sometimes to the point of squabbling—and I am always better off for it. Daniel Foster has helped me to correct my deficiencies in the realms of philosophy. Jonah Goldberg and I disagree on many of the questions that I deal with in these pages, and I have profited greatly from his willingness to debate them with me in good humor. Outside of *National Review*, I am indebted to Dana Perino, Ellen Carmichael, and Noah Rothman, all three of whom have offered invaluable pointers along the way.

For all the idle talk of "conservative echo chambers" and "right-wing bubbles," it will presumably come as no surprise to anybody who is half-switched-on that my particular brand of classical liberalism is not greeted with nodding heads and delighted cheers in either my country of birth or in the two vicinities in which I now spend most of my time: New York City and southern Connecticut. To propose earnestly in any of those places that individuals should be permitted to own military-grade firearms, that the established educational system is an authoritarian disaster, and that the answer to what ails America is a return to a thriving and diverse localism is, invariably, to be met with raised eyebrows. Far from being a burden, however, I consider this to be a considerable opportunity, and I am grateful to my friends and extended family for having forced me to hone my arguments.

Likewise, I am thankful that I had such open-minded and rigorous tutors at both school and university. At school, Robert Henderson, Christopher Bates, and Andrew Bamford were instrumental in instilling a love of history and politics at a young age. At Oxford, Clive Holmes taught me America's revolutionary history with flair and love, and Gillian Peele gave me a political education that I doubt could be matched. For better or for worse, their fingerprints are all over my case.

I have dedicated this book to my father, the best man I know. It is impossible to distill into a single paragraph what a parent gives to a child, so I will not try. Instead, I will merely say "thank you." Ultimately, all adults are kids pretending to be grown up, and, in consequence, it matters a great deal whose example they adopt for their simulation. I could not have been given a superior illustration or a better chance in this world. You are patient, caring, and fun, and you gave me my two great loves in life: music and debate. This volume is for you.

Index